Saint Martin
& Sint Maarten

Fodor's 90

Saint Martin & Sint Maarten

Julie Wilson

This book contains material previously published as
Fodor's Fun in St. Martin & St. Maarten.

FODOR'S TRAVEL PUBLICATIONS, INC.
New York & London

ISBN 0–679–01831–X

Fodor's Saint Martin & Sint Maarten

Editor: Denise Nolty
Drawings: Ted Burwell
Maps: Pictograph
Cover Photograph: M. Thonig/H. Armstrong Roberts

Cover Design: Vignelli Associates

Special Sales

Fodor's Travel Publications are available at special discounts for bulk
purchases (100 copies or more) for sales promotions or premiums. Special
editions, including personalized covers, excerpts of existing guides, and
corporate imprints, can be created in large quantities for special needs. For
more information, write to Special Marketing, Fodor's Travel Publications,
201 East 50th Street, New York, NY 10022. Enquiries from the United
Kingdom should be sent to Fodor's Travel Publications, 30–32 Bedford
Square, London WC1B 3SG.

Contents

Introduction

Every year nearly one million vacationers seek out this particular Caribbean island. They come by plane, charter yacht, and cruise ship to a tiny, 37-square-mile dot that lies due east of Puerto Rico, just at the point where the Caribbean Islands turn southward and start dropping like pebbles down to South America. Fortunately, they do not all come at the same time.

What they find is an island with nearly as many beaches as it has square miles. They find a green-peaked place whose hills are dotted with papayas, goats, palm trees, turk's head cactus, cows, and hibiscus. It's an island with flat, sandy arms that encompass Simpson Bay Lagoon, the largest inland body of water in the Caribbean and the best friend a fledgling water-sport enthusiast ever had. It's an island cooled by tradewinds—a place where the skies are not cloudy all day. Visitors find American breakfasts on this resort island that is often European in feeling. Beneath the international facade beats a pure Caribbean heart—rum in the sun, reggae on the radio, and a charmingly haphazard approach to life. Despite all there is to do, the slow pace winds you down faster than a watch with a sprung spring.

The island is the smallest land mass in the world to

contain two sovereign nations, Saint Martin and Sint Maart-
en. Visitors find France, Holland, and sun all for the price
of one ticket.

This political oddity has an early history much like any
other Caribbean island. Initially it was inhabited by peaceful
Arawak Indians and bloodthirsty Caribs, a cannibalistic clan
with a consuming interest in anyone who came ashore.
Then Columbus sailed by, naming the island San Martino
and prudently staying well offshore.

After the Indians were disposed of, a local version of
Capture the Flag ensued. The French, British, Dutch, and
Spanish arrived—anyone with a couple of ships and expan-
sionist ideas—and traded toeholds on the island. Pirates
also dropped in periodically.

Then the story changes. After everyone else went away,
those who remained were the Dutch (who were after the salt
on the island) and the French (who were after the Dutch).

Legend has it that the two armies, ignoring warlike
instructions from home, decided to lay down muskets and
settle the matter in a gentlemanly fashion. A Frenchman
and a Dutchman stood back to back on one shore (Point A)
and began marching around the perimeter. When they met
face to face (Point B), they drew the border, a nearly straight
line cutting across the hills, through the Lagoon, and over
the lowlands. The Dutchman, being rather portly and sipping Dutch gin all the way, didn't make very good time—
which explains why St. Maarten has 16 square miles of the
island and St. Martin has 21. For their capital, the Dutch
chose Philipsburg (named after John Philips, a Scotsman
employed by the Dutch West India Company). The French
chose Grand Case and then changed their minds and chose
Marigot.

These amicable armies left future generations the
problem of dealing with the unwieldy name of St. Martin/
St. Maarten—which is a lot less poetic than Pago-Pago,
Bora-Bora, or Bongo-Bongo. (The St. Martin/St. Maarten
order indicates no preference for one side over the other—
it's alphabetical.)

The legendary walk occurred 342 years ago. Today, the
border is nothing more than an invisible line you cross
without knowing it, unless you glance up at one of the signs
saying "Bienvenue Partie Française" or "Welkom aan de

Nederlandse Kant." In fact, there *is* a small border monument on the inland road behind Simpson Bay Lagoon.

This is not to say that the two sides have lost their separate identities. When the tourist tide started washing ashore some 35 years ago, the Dutch side was quicker than the French to see the possibilities. Consequently, it has most of the big hotels (in clusters), more sports facilities, more marinas, all the casinos, and the airport. The French side spreads its smaller attractions around more. And being very French, it has the lion's share—though not all—of the best restaurants. Happily, you don't have to choose sides: Whatever catches your fancy is no more than 20 minutes away from whatever beach you happen to be sitting on.

Despite the informality of that border, certain territorial formalities are maintained that add to the island's unique character. Local papers once reported the case of a nude swimmer who had been bitten by a fish on a previously unexposed part of his anatomy. When he complained to Dutch authorities, he was told that because he had been swimming off a French beach, he had been attacked by a French fish and should report the incident to the gendarmes. He was also advised to seek medical attention.

Aside from fierce (and probably provoked) minnows, the island is easygoing, with fun in the sun on its mind. It assiduously devotes itself to good food, good drink, and good times—and its most important border is the one on the sybaritic. The restaurant owners (about 200 of them) are constantly honing their knives and sharpening their sauces in delicious competition. At everything from ceremonial feasts to beach barbecues, rum (in a hundred different guises) and wine are the approved libations.

In between meals, there's all manner of water sports—snorkeling, swimming, sailing, scuba diving, and just sunning on all those beautiful beaches, in the Lagoon, and in the reef-ringed crystalline waters. The island is carved by small bays and coves. Beneath some placid surface waters lurk tricky undertows; beneath other placid surface waters, the water *is* placid.

In between everything else, there's shopping. With both sides having an enviable duty-free status, the island is a sunny bargain basement for European clothing, fine china and crystal, perfume, and liquor, and all those good things that make the good life worth living.

Finally, blessed with a location as convenient as its climate is benign, St. Martin/St. Maarten is a springboard for day trips to nearby islands. Hardly a pelican flight away, French St. Barts, Dutch St. Eustatius and Saba, and English Anguilla were also discovered by Columbus, who barely left one island before he bumped into the next.

General Information

"Eighty degrees and sunny" is pretty much a standard, year-round weather forecast down here. Cooling trade-winds ensure that it practically never gets muggy and sticky, and some evenings the breezes cool things down enough that you might want a light sweater. Basically, it's a dry island, washed by occasional brief but torrential down-pours.

Once upon a time there were clearly defined tourist "seasons," with high season starting in mid-December and ending by Easter. High season, however, has stretched, and the island operates near capacity from November right into early summer. Fortunately, hotels still operate under the old rules, so prices are lower "off" season. (Airlines don't; they charge peak season rates in July and August.)

Thanksgiving, Christmas, New Year's, and all of February are crowded. This is when the Beautiful People descend on the island, quickly followed by all their Beautiful Guests for rounds of entertaining and house parties. It's also a favorite time for families and for anyone with a bathing suit and the price of a plane ticket.

For many, the best month is June, when the flamboyant trees are in bloom, the crowds are elsewhere, and you can make a last-minute decision about dinner without worrying about reservations. A few hotels and restaurants close for September and October, the two months that are in the middle of hurricane season.

WHAT TO PACK

Lightweight, loose-fitting resort wear—the lighter-weight and looser-fitting the better. Island outfits run the gamut from elegantly informal to cut-off casual. Don't be too casual, though. Bathing suits and cover-ups are fine around the hotel, but decidedly tacky around town.

Jackets for gentlemen are not required anywhere, but you might feel more comfortable wearing one in some of the fancier restaurants. Though stopping well short of the tiara, some ladies get very dressed up in the evening. Some don't—it's really up to you. The best advice may be to bring anything that goes well with a sunburn.

Tennis racquet and snorkeling gear—They don't take up much room, and you'll probably be sorry if you leave them home, especially on the smaller islands where they might not be easily available.

Flashlight—Electrical power is relentlessly reliable on St. Martin/St. Maarten, but if you're going to spend the night on one of the smaller islands, you may be glad to have a flashlight along.

Travel alarm—Wake-up calls are unheard of in many places.

Converter—If you're staying on St. Martin, the voltage is 220 AC, 50 cycles, so you'll need French adapter plugs and a transformer for American-made hair dryers and electric shavers. No problem on the Dutch side, where the voltage is 110 AC, 60 cycles—just like home.

Film—If you have an older camera or use special film, bring what you need with you. Otherwise, standard film is readily available at the same price you pay at home. There's no got-'em-over-a-barrel mark-up on suntan lotion either. And, of course, French tanning creams and lotions are a duty-free bargain here.

A small duffel or tote bag—How else are you going to carry home all those duty-free bargains and pretty shells?

GETTING THERE

Both American Airlines and Pan American Airways have daily flights to St. Maarten from New York's JFK Airport; ALM has several flights a week. Eastern flies in daily from Miami, and Continental from Newark. American's daily flight from Dallas/Fort Worth, and Eastern's daily flight from Philadelphia, stop in San Juan, picking up passengers from connecting flights.

From Canada, BWIA (British West Indies Air) has Saturday flights from Toronto and American flies from Toronto and Montreal several times a week.

From San Juan, American Eagle and Eastern Express have daily flights. A number of smaller airlines, such as LIAT and Windward Islands Airways (WINAIR), connect St. Maarten with other Caribbean Islands.

ENTRY

To land on the island, you'll need the immigration card provided on the plane and one of the following—a valid passport, a passport that has expired within the past five years, a birth certificate, naturalization papers, or an Alien Registration ("Green") card. You'll also need to know where you're staying. And don't lose the carbon of that immigration card—you must surrender it on departure.

ARRIVAL

Regardless of which side of the island you're staying on, you'll arrive at St. Maarten's Princess Juliana Airport—unless you're sailing in or jumping a cruise ship. This modern, newly expanded airport is the second busiest (after Puerto Rico's San Juan) in the Caribbean. There are no customs formalities here, so once you've cleared the painfully slow-moving immigration process and found your bags, you're on your way.

There's a strong taxi drivers' union on the island. Therefore, even if you've rented a car, you can't pick it up here but must hire a cab to go to the hotel. The taxi situation appears to be chaotic—a melange of waving arms, frayed tempers, and people tripping over luggage. In fact, it's surprisingly orderly, with the unflappable dispatchers finding a cab for everyone in due time. Meanwhile, roll up your sleeves, turn your face to the sun, and start working on your tan. The islands move at their own pace.

There are no meters in the cabs; fares are government regulated. A price list is supposedly posted in the airport (just try and find it), and the dispatchers can tell you what a ride will cost. Recent fares: Marigot, $7; Philipsburg, $7; Grand Case, $13; Mullet Bay Resort, $4; The rate assumes that each cab carries two passengers and two suitcases. There are additional charges for additional passengers and luggage, and a surcharge after 10 P.M. Since overcharging is not unheard of, do get the right price from the dispatcher. If you're like 99 percent of the visitors to the island, you'll ask the driver, "How's the weather been?" He'll find that very funny.

DEPARTURE

Even though reconfirmation is no longer compulsory, it's still a wise idea to reconfirm 72 hours in advance. On a weekend in winter, there may be at least a half dozen people eyeing your space covetously. And airlines *do* overbook.

On the day of departure, the preferred procedure on this small island is to check in as early as possible and then spend the rest of the day on the beach, showing up at the last minute to waltz through the gate with your immigration card and $5 departure tax. This is fine except on holiday weekends (Thanksgiving, New Year's, and Washington's Birthday), when a number of charters and regular flights may be leaving at nearly the same time. Then you may run into two hours of shoving and exasperation just to get through immigration. The airport and airlines are trying to do something about it; meanwhile, be forewarned.

On the bright side, if you get there early, you can do some last-minute shopping for duty-free liquor, cigarettes, perfume, T-shirts, and Delft tiles. Or you can pass the time at Shimaruku Cafe Juliana, the airport's "sky club" bar/restaurant and the best thing to happen around here since they paved the runway.

TIME

The island operates on Atlantic standard time. If you're flying in from the East Coast in winter, set your watch ahead one hour; from the Midwest, ahead two hours.

LANGUAGE

French and Dutch are the official languages on the island, but aside from a few small shops and bistros on the French side, where the owners don't—or won't—speak English, English is the unofficial language. That lilting, incomprehensible language islanders speak among themselves is Papiamento, an Antillian dialect.

MONEY MATTERS

The French franc (approximately 6 to the dollar) and the Netherlands Antilles florin, or guilder (approximately 2 to the dollar), are the official currencies. The dollar is the accepted currency. Even if prices are listed in francs or guilders, you hand over dollars and—after a "blink of the eye" process of conversion and reconversion—get your change back in dollars. Major credit cards are widely accepted, and the price will always be converted into dollars.

There is a 5 percent room tax on both sides of the island and a 10–15 percent service charge. Some places add an "energy surcharge" for the use of air conditioners and/or fans.

There is no meal tax, but restaurants nearly always add a 15 percent service charge to the bill. If you're paying by credit card, you may find that 15 percent in the box labeled "tax," so watch it, unless you like leaving 30 percent tips.

GETTING AROUND

Taxis are easy to book from any hotel or restaurant, and the island bus connects Marigot, Philipsburg, Grand Case, and all the small towns in between. Buses run from 6 A.M. to midnight, and it costs only 85 cents for a leisurely ride and impromptu sightseeing tour.

For proper sightseeing tours, try St. Maarten Sightseeing (22753) or S.E.L. Maduro and Sons (23408) in Philipsburg, the St. Maarten Taxi Association (45329) in Cole Bay, or Dutch Tours at Cay Hill (23316). Tours take about 2½ hours and cost around $25 for two.

For $90 you can even take a bird's-eye tour of the island from Heli-Inter Caraïbes helicopter service, which is based at Anse Marcel (87–37–37).

Unless you plan to hole up in your hotel, however, you'll really need a car to explore all those beaches and to sample all those menus. Recognizing this, the islanders have established nearly as many car rental companies as there are rum drinks. Hertz, Avis, Budget, and others are represented here, though locally owned Risdon is far and away the largest. Rates start at about $42 a day for a basic automatic and go up with extras such as air-conditioning. Mopeds (about $20 a day) can be rented from Moped Cruising, N.V. (22520) or at your hotel.

You'll need an American driver's license to rent a car, and it's best to arrange the rental through your travel agent in advance. Cars are delivered to your hotel without charge.

For the most part, roads are good here (better on the French side), local drivers are good (if a little lead-footed), and everybody drives on the right (well, nearly everybody). Unless you spend an inordinate amount of time on the road, a tank of gas should last a week—it's a *very* small island.

WATER

The water is safe to drink, but it's also scarce. They don't use picturesque old cisterns as planters here, they use them as cisterns, and even the most exclusive, expensive hotels remind their guests to go easy on the showers. For a quick cool-down, the sea is free.

TELEPHONES

For an up-to-date island, St. Martin/St. Maarten sometimes seems only about 3½ weeks behind Alexander Graham Bell when it comes to the telephone. Calling within St. Martin is usually easy and calling within St. Maarten is sometimes easy. Calling between the two is a pain in the ear.

Remember these basics. All St. Maarten numbers have five digits and all St. Martin numbers have six digits (the first two of which are 87). To call from St. Martin to St. Maarten, dial 3, then the number. To call the other way, dial 06, plus the number.

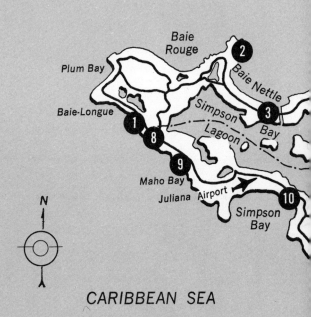

St. Martin/Sint Maarten

Baie
Rouge

Plum Bay

Baie Nettle

Baie-Longue

Simpson

Lagoon

Bay

Maho Bay

Juliana Airport

Simpson
Bay

N

CARIBBEAN SEA

Points of Interest

1) La Samanna
2) La Belle Creole
3) Le Santal
4) Le Poisson d'Or
5) La Nacelle
6) Grand Case Beach
7) L'Habitation

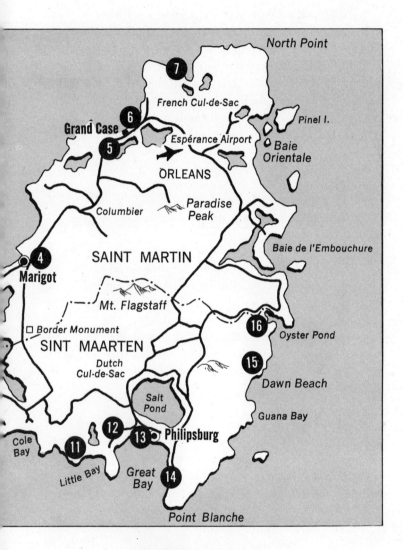

8) Mullet Bay
9) Maho Bay
10) Simpson Bay Village
11) Divi Little Bay Beach Hotel
12) Great Bay Beach Hotel and Casino
13) Front Street
14) Bobby's Marina/Great Bay Marina
15) Dawn Beach Hotel
16) Oyster Pond Hotel

And there's the problem. For some unfathomable Gallic reason, the French route all incoming and outgoing calls from St. Martin through Guadeloupe—which is rather like routing calls between Manhattan and Brooklyn through Prince Edward Island. It can be frustrating dialing a number yourself and expensive if you ask the hotel to do it, but give it a try. If a call doesn't go through, you can always get in the car and drive over to whomever you wanted to telephone.

OBVIOUS ADVICE

Leave the heavy-duty jewelry at home—you won't need it on this supercasual island. If you must bring valuables, store them (along with your passport and spare cash) in the safe deposit boxes available at most hotels.

Bring along a good supply of any medicines you need, including aspirin. A request for aspirin in a supermarket is likely to be met with a suspicious glare and the angry response, "We don't *do* drugs."

Lock your car.

Treat the sun with the same respect you would any run-of-the-mill inferno. These lovely beaches are only 18 degrees from the equator, and even if you think you never burn, you may be in for an uncomfortable surprise. Twenty minutes of prime-time rays are the limit for the first day—no kidding.

A few final words of caution: We have recently received reports from readers concerning an increase in petty crime on the island. While this should not deter you from visiting, you should take the same precautions you would anywhere else. Don't leave belongings unattended on a beach. Don't wander down dark alleys late at night. Don't inquire about the availability of "recreational drugs." And don't forget to use your safe deposit boxes.

THE VILLA ALTERNATIVE

The currently popular option of a rented home, an apartment, or other "self-catering accommodation" as an economical alternative to a hotel has been well established on the island for years. Options range from small, in-town apartments to luxury villas complete with pool and a gardener to sweep the hibiscus blossoms out of said pool. Options even include entire hotels, such as St. Maarten's Dawn Beach, or apartments in places as posh as St. Martin's La Samanna. The only thing they all have in common is a kitchen—it takes the financial sting out of breakfast and other informal meals.

Nearly all "villas" include maid service, and many are available for short-term (by the night) rental. St. Maarten's La Vista is a charming newcomer to these ranks. Overlooking Simpson Bay, it's a small hotel (done up in West Indian/ Nantucket style) with big rooms, big kitchens, and a big pool. Double rooms run from $225 to $250. (ITR Reservations, 800–223–9815 or 212–840–6636.)On St. Martin, Petite Plage—where Anguilla appears to be only a stone's throw from your breakfast table—is a small "motel," with kitchens, on a secluded beach. (Grand Case, 97150, St. Martin, FWI.)

For villa information about both sides of the island, contact Judy Shepherd at St. Maarten Rental, Pelican House, Beacon Hill, St. Maarten, NA (011–599–5–44330), Caribbean Concepts at 516–293–4900 (800–423–4433 toll-free), or ask your travel agent about villa-rental companies in the United States.

St. Martin

Aside from a few short detours down to one of the 32 beaches, up into the hills, or around the back of Simpson Bay Lagoon, the island's main road is essentially a circle. If you stand at one of the borders and just start walking, you'll be following in the footsteps of the legendary Frenchman and Dutchman. Of course, there are a lot more distractions along the way these days, so you might as well take a car.

If the Frenchman started his walk on the western border, he'd be in Basse Terre, the island's Gold Coast. Dotted with the well-secluded homes of wealthy Americans, Europeans, and islanders, it's got more *privée* signs than there are sand flies at sunset. Down its back roads are two of the island's quietest beaches, Plum and Rouge, which are backed by homes rather than hotels. Find them by driving as close to the water as possible until you come to the little public-access pathways. Paved driveways are *not* public-access pathways.

LODGING

It's quite fitting that the island's most exclusive (and well-known) hotel is located in Basse Terre. Starting on a cliff top, spilling down a hillside and along the beach, the mock-Moorish, pseudo-Hellenic, stage-set Beau Geste, **La Samanna** has been, for the past 15 years, the ultimate in vacation chic. It's so exclusive that there's no sign on the road. If you belong there, you know where it is.

All white walls and graceful arches, a tropical abundance of bougainvillea, a dazzle of Italian tiled pool and blue-striped umbrellas, La Samanna has a guest list that reads like the Powerful and Beautiful People Yearbook. At $640–$775 a night for two, it's what one might call expensive. But, of course, the tariff includes breakfast and dinner. Of course.

For that price, you get just what you'd expect—jealously guarded privacy (the kind you like if your name is Onassis, Redford, or Nixon), unobtrusive luxury, and an operation that runs as smoothly as an expensive Swiss watch. As if by magic, bouquets of hibiscus blossoms appear in the room each morning; ceiling fans circulate the breeze around; bathrooms gleam with colorful tiles; and in some of the upper rooms, the terraces are spacious enough to resemble the playing fields of Eton. Slip across your private patio and through a patch of sea grape trees and you're out on Long Beach, with its miles of pristine shoreline that are overlooked by a few privileged, obsessively private homes. La Samanna's restaurant is one of the best on the island (see *Restaurants*) and after dinner everyone repairs to the bar, where they roll the tapes for a little dancing chic-to-chic under the festive Indian canopy. (David B. Mitchell & Co., telephone 212–696–1323.)

The road between Basse Terre and Marigot seems to have suddenly exploded with new buildings along Nettle Bay. Apart from all this, out on Pointe des Pierres à Chaux, stands **La Belle Creole.** Spending most of the past 20 years as an impossibly glamorous, half-finished ghost town—a cautionary tale about vaulting ambition and insufficient financing—La Belle Creole scheduled opening after opening and canceled them all. It finally opened last year and seems—at last—to be shifting into high gear. Early reports laud the 156 rooms, the restaurants, the three beaches, and a pleasant staff who are absolutely delighted to welcome guests. With its piazzalike center courtyard, narrow alleyways, and old stone buildings, La Belle Creole looks like a Mediterranean village. Well, that was the idea. Doubles run from $235 to $515. (Hilton Reservation Services, telephone 800–HILTONS.)

MARIGOT

Marigot, St. Martin's capital, is a harbor town with a distinctly Gallic flavor, full of small cafés and serious restaurants. It's also pure St. Martin, with picturesque West Indian homes, deep drainage ditches between sidewalk and street, and a plethora of duty-free shops. Historically quiet and *intime,* it has recently burst into a frenzy of building and, while the developers forgot to provide parking places, they did manage to post a multitude of one-way street signs.

Marigot's heart is at the harbor. Every morning, overseen by Marigot's recently restored Fort St. Louis, the market comes alive (more alive on Saturday than any other day). Passengers mingle for the early morning boat to Anguilla. Rickety stalls bend under the weight of bananas, yams, small green limes, a colorful array of gasping fish, writhing masses of naked conch, and Haitian bric-a-brac. In the midst of the hubbub, the doors of the helpful St. Martin Tourist Information Bureau, housed in a West Indian cabin designed by artist Roland Richardson, are open to visitors needing information and assistance.

DINING

Waterfront restaurants are shuttered at the market's hour of morning, except for **La Vie En Rose** on the corner of Rue de la République. Here you can nibble on a fresh-baked pastry, sip a cup of coffee, and watch the world, Marigot-style, go about its business. Following the harbor's curve westward, you'll come to **Le Bar de la Mer,** which also serves morning coffee and pastries, along with light lunches and suppers—and pastis with a smile in the late afternoon.

On the town's lagoon shore, Port La Royale Marina is a still-growing development of condominiums and boutiques, with a smattering of small international bistros. You can check on the health and breakfast habits of many of St. Martin's restaurant owners when they show up daily at Port La Royale's terrace cafe **Mastedana** across from the cemetery. Roger Druoin (an advertising executive who abandoned the fast life of Montreal for the fresh air of Marigot) and his entire family serve up the island's best croissants and coffee. For inexpensive Italian dishes, **Don Camillo** is the best bet, **Cafe de Paris** is *the* place to be seen sipping coffee these days, and **Etna Ice Cream Per Dolce Vita** serves terrific home-made ice creams and sherberts.

For a taste of preboom Marigot, find **Chez Max** on Waterloo Alley. Have an early morning coffee with the gendarmes and fishermen and come back later for the best court bouillon de poisson on the island.

LODGING

Right in town, the 20-room **La Résidence** is a sweet bijou of a city hotel, with plenty of charm to make up for the absence of beaches. Its second-floor dining courtyard has a bubbling fish fountain, friendly bar, and swag curtains around some secluded tables. Doubles with breakfast start at $100. (WIMCO, telephone 401–849–8012 or 800–932–3222.) **Hotel Royale Louisiana,** just down the street, is brand new, all sparkling green and white—and a bit more expensive. Doubles are currently $110, including breakfast. (Accor International, telephone 914–472–0370 or 800–221 –4542.)

Don't be put off by the preliminaries of getting to **Club Le Grand Beach Resort** on the far side of town—you can only get there down a number of zigzagging back alleys. It's actually right on the beach, Galisbay and Potence Beach to be precise, where they used to hang and bury miscreants in the old days. It's all very relaxed here, at the island's first all-inclusive (a room, three meals, water sports, and an enormous swimming pool) resort. Rates are $300–$375 a night for two. (Mars Leisure Corporation, telephone 800– 221–1831 or 201–842–7677.)

GRAND CASE

After Marigot, the road starts climbing uphill and down through little towns (actually no more than a handful of houses, a bar, and a bakery) until you're in Grand Case—a veritable Restaurant Row.

To ease stupendous traffic jams, Grand Case recently built a ring road on its inland side, but for all intents and purposes, this is still a one-street town. It's a scant, amiable half-mile lined with fabulous restaurants that can best be divided into those that are on the waterfront and those that are not. Just park the car and walk, sniff, and read menus, occasionally glancing over at Anguilla in the near distance.

If you tear your eyes away from the menus, you'll see that Grand Case looks for all the world like a small Mediter-ranean port on a picture postcard. A few yachts and small boats bob in the harbor, which is embraced on three sides by green hills. There's a fisherman's pier, a few small guest houses, and a few houses along the beach that are not yet restaurants. Give them time.

Behind the town, the island's "other" airport is a tidy little operation with the wing-and-a-prayer name of L'Esp-érance. It's used mainly by private planes, but Air Guadeloupe does have regularly scheduled flights to St. Barts from here. (About $25 per person, one way.)

LODGING

At the far end of the town's beach stands the **Grand Case Beach Club,** a row of two- and three-story buildings partly screened by sea grape trees. You'll find a mixed group here—young couples, older couples, people who settle in for months at a time. It's very much a club, and you can be as reclusive or as convivial as you want. Sooner or later, though, you'll probably get to know all the other guest/members.

For $175–$215 a night, every room has a well-equipped galley kitchen, every room has a private porch; and nearly every room overlooks the bay. ("Garden" rooms overlook the parking lot.) There's an affable water-sports center, and the restaurant *Waves* is set on a rocky ledge away from the rooms, so at night the only sound you hear is the gentle lapping of the real waves. (Reservations Systems Inc., telephone 212–661–4540 or 800–223–1588.)

Besides possessing a fair share of Grand Case Beach, the Club also shares a secluded little beach around the corner with **Petite Plage.** Screened from the beach by a tangle of trees and bushes, Petite Plage has six simply furnished suites ($110–$175), each with its own patio and kitchenette. It's enchanting, very private, and always booked. Your best chance here is to contact owner Roger Laurence and hope for a cancellation. (Telephone 305–666–4083.)

Most of the local accommodations are on the same small, casual scale and perfectly suited to this small, casual town in which where you eat is more important than where you sleep. Little **Hevea** is nearly an afterthought to a splendid restaurant of the same name. (Caribbean Concepts, telephone 516–293–4900 or 800–423–4433). At **Chez Martine,** the water's-edge restaurant draws more attention than the hotel's eight basic rooms. (Chez Martine, Grand Case, 97150, St. Martin, FWI.)

The new kid on the block—and on the beach—is **La**

Belle Grand Case, a collection of eight comfortable apartments grouped around a central staircase. The staff like guests so much that they give them not only a complimentary bottle of champagne, but a bottle of wine as well. Such hospitality! Rates are about $800 to $2,000 a week, but even the smallest studio sleeps three. (Landmark Travel, telephone 617–893–4111.)

Up in the hills just out of town, tiny **Bertine's** is a barefoot sort of place with five rooms and the ambience of a European guest house. There's little to do up here but sit under the tamarind tree, admire the view, breathe clean air, check on the ripening mangoes, and listen to the quiet. At night, Chicago-born owner Bernard Poticha turns chef, serving Creole snapper, chocolate mousse pie, and barbecued ribs Chicago-style. (Bertine's, Savana, Grand Case, St. Martin, FWI. 87–58–39.)

After Grand Case, the road swings around the top of the island, where cows outnumber the cars, then through French Quarter on the way to Orleans. From mid-afternoon on, the views from these hills are a photographer's dream.

In between photographs, take a left at French Cul de Sac to **L'Habitation.** St. Martin's biggest (201 rooms, 52 apartments) hotel, it occupies all of Anse Marcel, known for its remote beauty and its snorkeling. The style is vaguely "Creole Plantation," and the facilities ambitious—two restaurants, 25 boutiques, a big pool, a marina, charter yachts, and a marble lobby that would be right at home in any palace. Afternoon tea and evening entertainment, with the delightfully named Orville Roach at the piano, are added attractions. Doubles run from $284 to $336. (Mondotels, telephone 212–757–0225 or 800–847–4249.)

Le Club Privilège, up the hill, is L'Habitation's all-purpose sports center with tennis courts, squash courts, archery, pool, open-air gym, aerobic studio, and a couple of restaurants for refueling. If that's not enough exercise, the disco rocks until dawn.

Before the somnolent hamlet of Orleans—where St. Martin's best-known artist, Roland Richardson, has his studio—a road off to the left leads down to breezy, white-sanded Orient Beach, and the **Club Orient.** If you're a "naturist" you've probably already heard of Club Orient, the only no-clothes resort in the Caribbean. If you're not, this is the place to discover if you might like to be. They're very accommodating about their "free beach" and understanding about the fact that the shedding of bathing suits requires a certain shedding of inhibitions. If you want just to enjoy this mostly deserted Atlantic beach and keep your clothes on, that's fine, too.

The hotel itself draws a smattering of Europeans and a lot of families. The 75 pinewood chalets (doubles $125–$175) look like they belong on a Finnish lake surrounded by birch trees rather than on a Caribbean beach surrounded by turk's head cactus. There's not a sauna in sight, but there are a small beachfront restaurant, a water-sports center, and some fine swimming in the reef-protected waters. It's really quiet here, with an end-of-the-world feeling. (Caribbean Hideaways, telephone 914–733–4596 or 800–828–9356.)

The end of the world, however, is shared with **Le Galion,** just over the hill on Baie de L'Embouchure. This has one of the calmest, most protected beaches on the island, a great placid pond perfect for swimming laps without the distraction of tumbling surf. However, distraction may come from the masses of cruise-ship passengers who stage periodic invasions.

Le Galion, whose 54 basically furnished rooms are strung along the beach, has always had a somewhat raffish ambience. Some recent sour notices, however, indicate it may be carrying this raffish bit too far and needs a shake-up. Doubles are $130 to $175. (Robert Reid Reservations Center, telephone 800–223–6510. American/Wolfe International, telephone 914–833–3303 or 800–223–5695. ITR, telephone 212–545–8469 or 800–223–9815.)

And after passing through the rest of the French Quarter, past flower-tangled stone walls, more cows, and the new construction of another French building spree, you'll come to the border of St. Maarten and to **Hotel Captain Oliver.**

In the spirit of local cooperation, Captain Oliver's spiffy marina docks and restaurant are on Dutch waters while his 25 hotel bungalows are on French soil. Heaven knows who does his bookkeeping. Doubles are $200–$300. Ask for one of the "sea view" rooms perched on a rocky cliff with a view of St. Barts. Then pull up a peacock chair on the

restaurant deck, order a beer or a meal, and consider the
delightful peculiarities of a two-nation island. (Pullman International Hotels, telephone 800–223–9862 or 212–757–
6500.)

St. Maarten

Starting the Dutchman's walk from the western border, you head toward the Lowlands of St. Maarten, a cove-carved narrow strip of land skirting Simpson Bay Lagoon. On the other side of the road are fine ocean beaches, clusters of hotels, and the airport.

LODGING

High on Simpson Bay Bluff, overlooking the Lowlands and Simpson Bay Lagoon, the **Summit** is one of the Dutch side's smaller (60 rooms) hotels. White buildings with half-timbering give it an Elizabethan appearance, but the palm trees and bougainvillea along the pathways are pure Caribbean. It's a little out of the way, has only one "all-weather" tennis court, and a small, lagoon-side beach reached by a steep flight of steps. But it has a great deal of lazy charm, and a super pool deck off the dining room with a bar, cooling breezes, and panoramic views. You'll find a young crowd here (some with well-behaved children), and a fair number of singles. (Doubles $100–$140. Resort Sales Counsel, telephone 203–847–9445 or 800–622–7836.)

Down the hill, **Treasure Island Hotel and Casino at Cupecoy,** is one of St. Maarten's largest resorts (366 rooms). A Mediterranean fantasy of curved arches and freshly painted white walls, it overlooks a powder-sand beach, where centuries of wind and wave have carved little niches and grottoes into the pink sandstone cliffs. Interior courtyards contain a veritable botanical garden of carefully tended plants, an all-purpose dining room, and a large pool. This pool has the added attraction of a swim-up bar, complete with underwater bar stools. The perfect place for a Mark Spritzer.

One caveat: The best rooms are along the cliff (doubles $275–$350 per night) and those overlooking the gardens. The "standard" rooms are across the road in a massive development with the Treasure Island casino, restaurant, shopping piazza, and outdoor breakfast buffet. If you're going, specify the "Beach Club." (Caribbean Reservations, telephone 609–484–0020 or 800–535–2929.)

Next stop on the road is the enormous **Mullet Bay Resort**—a self-sufficient kingdom unto itself. Six hundred rooms are scattered in two-story units across 172 acres of prime real estate that meanders between the lagoon and one of the island's prettiest beaches. Originally built with some of the Ford millions, it had a few down years, but currently seems to be on an upswing—and certainly on a redecorating kick. Although current prices ($185–$280 for a double) are also on the upswing, you get a lot for your money. You get two pools, 14 tennis courts, the best water-sports center around, and a branch of the Chase Manhattan Bank. You get seven restaurants (they use some 3,000 eggs a day), a casino, a disco, and Mullet buses to trundle you from pleasure to pleasure to meeting rooms. You get count-less boutiques, a shopping mall, and the island's only golf course. You get that beach. And if the surf turns rough (as it sometimes does) and the red flags go up, you just amble on up to the bar for a rum punch. Life is easy here.

Mullet is not designed for the adventuresome. The rooms are air-conditioned rather than ceiling-fanned, and the chances of your finding a little yellow bird swooping through your louvers are more than remote. The restaurants are suited to American steak, ice cream, and deli tastes. But this is the place to be if you don't feel like trekking all over the island in search of fun: Fun is right here. (GEM Marketing, telephone 212–593–8600 or 800–4–MULLET.)

Just next to Mullet, elbow-roomy **Maho Beach Hotel and Casino** has a lobby the size of a football field, great swooping beams that hold up the ceilings, big rooms, and big spenders in the casino. It's got a big pool and four standard-size tennis courts. Maho attracts a lot of tours and a lot of young people. The disco and casino are now located in an enormous new complex across the road. Doubles are $150–$290. (Sea and Sun Holidays, telephone 800–223–0757 or 212–969–9220.)

Tucked into a corner of Maho's beach (if a 108-unit hotel can be tucked into anything), **La Plage at Royal Islander Club** is the newest luxury hotel in these parts—acres of Italian marble, windows on the water, microwaves in private kitchens, and so on. Rates are $165–$280. La Plage shares Maho's casino, shopping arcade, and beach. (Sun and Sea Holidays, telephone 800–223–0757 or 212–969–9244.)

Located at the end of the airport runway, this beach is a fascinating place to be when you're lying on your back looking up at the underbellies of small planes wobbling in for a landing. It's another story when the jumbos come in, bearing down like giant pterodactyls and the sand swirls around like a climactic scene from *Lawrence of Arabia*.

Anchoring down the other end of this exciting beach and marked by the sign of the mythical griffin, **The Caravanserai** harks back to the beginnings of tourism on the island. At one time, it was mentioned in the same breath as Raffles and the Mandarin. The growth of the airport and a partnership with Mullet Bay have taken the edge off its aura of remoteness. Nevertheless, it maintains a certain ingrained gentility and grace.

Banning all small children, the Caravanserai draws honeymooners and a return crowd of regulars who simply wouldn't stay anywhere else. They come for the two swimming pools (one with a griffin painted on the bottom), a tiny gemlike beach, afternoon tea in the Palm Court, and an octagonal dining room perched on a craggy coral outcropping, with the island's best views of Saba and the sunsets. Doubles are $185–$270. (GEM Marketing, telephone 212–593–8600 or 800–642–6401.)

Though in many respects it's a little "out of the way" inn on Simpson Bay, you can spot **Mary's Boon** as the plane is landing. Someone has painted the name on the roof. Just a few hundred yards from the central runway, it's got a dozen rooms in stilt-supported bungalows, and a quirky personality. The entrance is guarded by two life-size, painted British guardsmen. Doubles are $130. (Jane Conden, telephone 212–986–4373 or 800–223–5608.)

Beyond the end of the airport runway, a desultory road hooks back to Simpson Bay Village, the last "undiscovered" hamlet on the island. It's more Saba than St. Maarten out here, a small fishing village where neat little homes have neat little vegetable gardens in the yard and the church is named Mary Star of the Sea.

Down a dead-end street, **The Horny Toad** is a small guest house with eight apartments. It's laid-back, quintessentially old-time Caribbean, and has its own beach. The guests, for the most part, are loyal returnees, who know a good thing when they've found it. Apartments are $150 a night. (Dave and Betty Harvey, telephone 617–729–3171.)

Back on the beaten track, the Lowlands suddenly end at Cole Bay, where the main road turns right at a congested corner and climbs its twisting way up Cole Bay Hill before starting the descent to Philipsburg. There's a lookout point up here with great views of neighboring islands and a roadside refreshment stand aptly named Prime View.

At the bottom of the hill is the island's major supermarket, Food Center, which carries anything (except aspirin and couture fashions) you might want. You can put together a great picnic of bread, cheese, wine, and chocolate. And it's also the best place to buy Dutch chocolate and wheels of cheese to take home. (Closed Sunday and Monday mornings.)

Just before Philipsburg, the road slices off again to the right, to the peninsula where Fort Amsterdam stands. For many years, it was a quiet ruin, best known as the place where Peter Stuyvesant lost his leg trying to wrest the island from the Spanish in 1644. Recently, it's been the center of some controversy, as developers ripped up the surrounding grounds to construct a time-sharing operation. The developers, it is rumored, plan to preserve as much of the fort as is possible.

LODGING

Thirty-five years ago, when the government decided to get into the hotel business, it prudently chose the best beach around—which is near the fort—and constructed a charming little beach resort. Now known as **Divi Little Bay Beach Hotel,** it's not so little any more (155 rooms), but it's still charming under a fresh coat of paint. Doubles today are $215–230.

The swimming and waterskiing are exceptionally good here, as is the sailing on a calm bay blessed with unpredictable wind gusts. (Divi Hotels, telephone 800–367–3484 or 607–277–3484.)

Just next door, the **Belair Beach Hotel** shares the bay and the water-sports facilities. Its two-bedroom suites ($195–$475) each possess a TV, kitchen, and private terrace with sea views framed by Moorish arches. Another attraction is La Grenouille, one of Philipsburg's best restaurants for years, which has moved out here to Belair. (Resort Sales Counsel, telephone 203–847–6377 or 800–622–7836.)

Moving back toward town, you come to **Great Bay Beach Hotel and Casino**—all glittery and glitzy and a favorite among gambling junketeers. Because gambling junketeers seldom stray far from the tables, the hotel has everything you might need, including a pool, beach, nightclub, and hairdresser. Doubles are $130–$195. (Sea and Sun Holidays, telephone 800–223–0757 or 212–969–9220.)

PHILIPSBURG

Philipsburg, St. Maarten's capital, is hardly your sleepy Caribbean village. In fact, it's very much a city, complete with proper traffic jams and a high energy level. The streets are narrow and you step off the sidewalk at your own peril. (Actually, remaining on the sidewalk is no guarantee of safety, since drivers have a somewhat loose notion as to the proper place for motor vehicles.) The streets are also crowded with pedestrians, and when cruise ships disgorge their hordes, the streets are very crowded indeed. Jammed full of duty-free shops, punctuated by plenty of places to eat and drink, Philipsburg resembles nothing so much as one giant shopping mall. But it's got a cocky vitality about it—and, just so you shouldn't take anything for granted, parts of it are constantly under construction.

The town takes up a narrow isthmus dividing Great Bay from Great Salt Pond. Not long ago, Philipsburg consisted of two streets—Front Street and Back Street—connected by tiny *steegjes*, no more than alleys. The streets were so crowded that the town filled in part of Salt Pond and made a new road called variously Pondfill Road, Ring Road, and "the new street." Still, Front Street and Back Street are not noticeably less crowded now.

Since there is no way for the town to expand laterally (pond filling being a tedious process), it's expanding at either end. And it's expanding up. Not far up, but up at last count, to a sky scraping seven stories. With all the new building going on, a lot of the beautiful old colonial architecture—with its fancy fretwork and gingerbread verandahs—has disappeared. But enough remains to distinguish Philipsburg from just another small city.

One of the most delightful examples to remain is the Courthouse (clearly labeled "Courthouse") on De Ruyterplein, in the center of town. It's not gingerbready, but solid, squat, and severe, as befits a responsible courthouse that's been here since 1793. The ground floor now houses the post office. At the other end of De Ruyterplein, Little Pier accommodates many of the sightseeing boats and boats heading for nearby islands. And next to Little Pier, the St. Maarten Tourist Office stocks brochures on nearly everything there is to do or see on the Dutch side of the island, and some information on the French side as well.

One of the best things to happen here in years is the recently opened St. Maarten Museum on Front Street. Located in a 19th-century "gingerbread" cottage, it's an admirable attempt by the islanders to share their West Indian heritage and culture. There is a "museum arcade" of shops being constructed around the cottage.

LODGING

As befits a major town, Philipsburg offers plenty of places to stay—big hotels, small hotels, beachfront apartments, guest houses—but there's no camping on the beach. One charming alternative, **The Pasanggrahan** (which means "guest house" in Indonesian) is the island's oldest hotel, nearly lost in the Front Street shuffle. A throwback to a more gracious era, it's got peacock chairs in the lobby and a portrait of Queen Wilhelmina on the wall. With only a couple of dozen ceiling-fanned rooms ($95–$125), a beachside bistro, tropical gardens, and the Sidney Greenstreet Bar, it qualifies as an oasis.

Blithely ignoring the bustle beyond its walls (but occasionally peeking out to make sure it's still there) The Pasanggrahan is the best place for the best of all worlds. Naturally, it serves afternoon tea. (ITR, telephone 212–545 –8469 or 800–223–9815.)

At the other end of the scale, the 78 room **Holland House** resembles a European businessman's hotel—right down to KLM posters of the Netherlands on the walls and the coffee shop just off the lobby. It is, in fact, a businessman's hotel, attracting briefcase carriers who appreciate efficiency and the fact that not everyone operates at the island's slow pace. The beach, however, is pure Caribbean. Doubles are $110–$145. (ITR, telephone 800–223–9815 or 212–545–8469.)

Nearby, the four-story **St. Maarten Beach Club and Casino** spreads across both sides of Front Street. As a city

hotel, it, too, draws business travelers. It also attracts vacationers who want kitchenettes, the convenience of being in
town, big rooms, and a lot of action on the doorstep. At the
Monday night cocktail party and steel band fête, there's
sometimes a man who eats glass and walks on nails. Now
that's action. Rooms here are $150–$175. (In the U.S., call
800–322–6990 or 312–427–2707.)

The St. Maarten Beach Club's lobby is one of Philipsburg's most popular meeting spots, the "lobby" being a
tropical rain forest of hanging plants and bamboo in which
a boisterous macaw and a relatively sedate cockatoo reside.
The "lobby" is also the Fandango Restaurant, open from
morning to night, with the island's largest menu (fried potato skins to surf 'n turf). And the lobby is the Heartbreak
Hotel Bar, where the rum punch could, well, break your
heart.

DINING

For an impromptu picnic on Great Bay Beach, **Café
Royal** in Royal Palm Plaza stuffs all manner of goodies from
pâtés to pastries, roast duck to Edam, into picnic baskets
that cost about $30 for two; they could serve four. If you
really want to make a production of your picnic, the café will
rent you a beach umbrella, beach bag, and cooler. The café
is open for breakfast and lunch and is one of the few places
on this side of the Atlantic where you can get a real Dutch
uitsmyter—two eggs and ham, roast beef, or cheese on toast.
(Telephone 23443.)

For smaller fare, grab an ice cream cone and a soda
from one of the "wagon carts" along Front Street and in the
arcades.

Way up at the top of Front Street, and on the way to
Point Blanche, **Bobby's Marina** and **Great Bay Marina** constitute the yachting center of the island. There are private
yachts up here, charter yachts, and most of the day sailers.
It's a great place for wandering and watching people mess
around with boats. Even if you're not a yachtsman, you'll
soon feel you are.

Out of Philipsburg, drive around the back of Salt Pond,

past the pastel-painted Amsterdam Shopping Center, up through residential Prince's Quarter, along some dusty back roads, then down a steep, winding mountain road that looks for all the world like a cement ribbon dropped off a cliff. You have found the most remote corner of St. Maarten.

Waves crash on a ring of far-off reefs, Atlantic breezes zip along, and St. Barts looks close enough to peek in the windows. There's a feeling of being cut off from the rest of the island, and—with that mountain road in mind—indeed you are. Just you, some houses mushrooming on the surrounding hills, a marina, and two hotels.

LODGING

The larger of the two hotels, **Dawn Beach Hotel,** has 155 units ($199–$275) sprinkled along the beach and up on the hillside. Each has a kitchenette and tropical motif furnishings. They do a lot to entertain you at Dawn Beach— Happy Hours, Sunday Brunches, barbecues, West Indian "Jump-Ups"—probably on the theory that you're not going anywhere anyway. If you tire of the beach, there's also a pool, bar, restaurant, and tennis courts. (ITR, telephone 800–223–9815 or 212–545–8469.)

Aside from having someone occasionally play the grand piano in the bar and serving memorable meals (see *Restaurants*), **Oyster Pond Yacht Club** does very little to entertain you. Paper hats and limbo dancers would be ludicrously out of place here.

One of the most beautiful hotels anywhere in the world, the Yacht Club sits like a fortress at the end of a peninsula, guarding both one end of Dawn Beach and the "hurricane hole" of Oyster Pond. The 20 rooms surrounding the circular courtyard are all named after ships ("I'm going for a nap in *Nirvana*"), and the white wicker furnishings are from France's Jacques Pergay. The antique accessories come from the Left Bank, the Galapagos Islands, and other far-flung places.

You can swim, snorkel, water-ski, sail, and race around

the tennis courts here. You can splash in the new pool. You can also read, eat, and simply enjoy the quiet.

Oyster Pond attracts people who want perfection and don't mind paying for it (rooms run $320–$360 a night). There's nothing stuffy about the hotel, however. Manager Suzanne Seitz (who once ran Haiti's legendary Grand Hotel Oloffson) sees that everyone, regardless of age or status, has the best time possible in Paradise. (David B. Mitchell, telephone 212–696–1323 or 800–372–1323.)

Restaurants

Whether it is the fact that this is a two-nation island—with all the competition and creative friction that implies—or whether it was some accidental confluence of good cooks, restaurant food here is superb. It's French, American, and Italian—with a dash of Creole, a whiff of East India, and an echo of the Orient. With 200 restaurants jammed into 37 square miles, it's a wonder that anyone manages to fit into a bathing suit after a few days.

The variety of available comestibles is somewhat astounding when you consider both the usual lackluster standard of island food and the fact that nearly everything but the odd lime and the occasional passing fish has to be imported.

And import they do. While the ubiquitous Caribbean trio of grouper (merou), red snapper (vivanneau), and langouste anchor many a menu, you'll also find Dover sole, Long Island duckling, Italian truffles, kosher pickles, and French *foie gras*, to say nothing of french fries. And though a quick tour of the Marigot market indicates a preponderance of bananas, yams, and dasheens, restaurants manage to corner a good supply of fresh vegetables and fruits, from ripe avocados to fresh strawberries.

As on all Caribbean islands, what you'll probably drink is rum—in piña coladas, rum and Coke, rum and tonic, rum punches, rum sundowners, and rum mumbles. Not surprisingly, Holland's Heineken is the easiest beer to find on both sides of this island. And the wines are French. French wines, however, are not particularly cheap in restaurants. Prices are comparable to those back home.

Most restaurants are still centered in Grand Case, Philipsburg, and Marigot. But these days it seems that every side road has at least one good restaurant, along with the requisite 17 potholes.

Don't overlook hotel restaurants. On this island, just about all of them are quite good and places to remember when you're too sunburned from a day of snorkeling to get in the car and drive anywhere. Mullet Bay's seven eateries, for example, constitute a veritable smorgasbord—with palatable prices. And some hotel restaurants stand head and sauces above anything else in the neighborhood.

At the height of the season, you need reservations just about everywhere. Some restaurants close down or work a shorter week during the summer, so check first. A large number of restaurants accept credit cards, and a 15 percent service charge is usually included on the bill.

THE BIG SIX

These are the places that everyone is going to ask you if you've been to when you get home—the places for memorable meals. Any one could lay claim to being the best restaurant on the island, and on any given day, it just might be. They all have the kind of flair, imagination, and commitment to excellence that have given St. Martin/St. Maarten its reputation. Just scrape the sand off your Gold Card, polish your best sandals, and go to any one of them.

To no one's surprise, one of the Big Six is the restaurant at **La Samanna.** From the day the dining room opened, it has set the standard for everyone else. Over a decade later, the place shows no signs of ennui—it's spectacular. (Telephone 87–51–22.)

The open dining room culminates in a porch overlooking the sea. Well-bred bananaquits twitter in the trees at lunch. The stars beam down discreetly at night. Tables are covered with linens of La Samanna's hallmark blue. The staff is all seeing and unobtrusive.

On weekly flights from France come such morsels as mussels, crayfish, or still-quivering scallops and roe. The produce of Rungis—baby carrots, slender beans, tiny turnips, fresh herbs—arrives in the kitchen at the same moment. Menu highlights include a crisp-skinned grilled red snapper with a green creole sauce, a feather-light broccoli terrine resting on a pink pool of lobster sauce, or an artistic rendition of sweetbreads and lobster with curry and courgettes. And at lunch, try the ultimate steak tartare.

As uncompromisingly uncompromising in its menu as in everything else, La Samanna doesn't bother to list its prices in dollars—it's francs only, which gets you used to numbers like 300 or 500. The translation comes to about $150 for two at dinner (with a modest bottle of wine) or about $50 for a bare-bones lunch. It's well worth it; don't miss it, if only to say you've been there.

On the opposite side of the island, the **Oyster Pond Yacht Club's** stylish restaurant makes the long trip worthwhile.

If you're looking for bright lights, brass bands, and blue cheese on the iceberg lettuce, go elsewhere.

It's quiet out here—just the sound of the waves, the rustle of palm fronds in the breeze, the sound of someone playing the piano in the bar, and the appreciative murmurs of your fellow diners. At lunch time, ask for a table in the courtyard, where you can sip your lobster-laced cold cucumber soup or nibble your duck breast salad at English teak tables. Evenings in the open dining room are more formal and more ambitious—avocado and smoked fish salad, lobster *noisettes* bathed in ginger butter, and all tantalizing pairings and nuances of fine cooking at its best.

The price tag for all this is just what it should be—dinners run over $100 for two and lunches about $40. As befits a small, personal-service hotel, however, they're flexible out here. They'll even cook you a cheeseburger if you want it—but why in the world would you? (Telephone 22206 or 23206.)

Opposite the pier in Grand Case, **La Nacelle** looks for all the world like an oversized birthday cake—all pink and white and West Indian architectural furbelows. It is (*quelle surprise*) the former *gendarmerie*. All police stations should come to such a happy end.

The restaurant is masterminded by Charles Chevillot, who also runs Manhattan's La Petite Ferme and Les Tournebroches. Chevillot's brother runs the Hotel de la Poste in Beaune, France.

Inside, the restaurant is airy, with ceiling fans and balloon prints on the walls (a *nacelle* being the little basket balloonists ride in). Outside, there's a spacious garden under almond trees reserved for predinner drinks and after-dinner coffee. The short menu, which changes daily, isn't as horrifyingly expensive as you might anticipate. Cool cucumber soup, lobster collops poached in Chablis, and a pear tart are among the frequently encountered delights. The staff is young, pleasant, and fiercely dedicated. Dinner only, and only in season. (Telephone 87–53–63.)

At over $110 for two, Marigot's **Le Poisson d'Or** isn't the most expensive restaurant on the island, but it's near enough, and worth every single sou. Beneath the candlelit dining verandah, bay waters lap quietly against the foundations of the 200-year-old building. The interior rooms are cool behind two-foot-thick stone walls. Artist Roland Richardson uses the walls as an art gallery, displaying both his own works and those of other talented local painters.

The presentation on the elegant Villeroy & Boch plates is as artistic as anything on the walls. House salad is no randomly tossed affair, but a platter of overlapping vegetables—sliced impossibly thin—with an eye to color, texture, and flavor. Sliced lobster spills out of an upturned carapace into a basil-flecked, bisquelike sauce. Local fish is smoked in the kitchen. And the chef's special dessert is rightly called an *"indulgent au chocolat."* (Telephone 87–50–33.)

Youngest of the smart-set restaurants, Philipsburg's **Le Bec Fin** overlooks Great Bay and is located directly behind the 100-year-old cottage donated by the restaurant's owner, Christian Cartayrade, to the new St. Maarten Museum.

Once you stop admiring the view and look at the menu, you'll realize this is a serious restaurant, serving fine food at its most imaginative. Gold stars on the menu go to chunks of lobster in puff pastry, served over spinach mousse and lobster sauce, and to red snapper with a saffron sauce. Have some of the restaurant's carrot "cake" (really more of a timbale) and top it all off with a Napoleon and fresh French strawberries with cassis. Your wallet, at the end of this exercise, will be lighter by some $125. Le Bec Fin is open daily for lunch and dinner. (Telephone 22976.)

Oldest of the six is **Le Santal,** which has hewn to its own impossibly high standards for over a decade. Down a dusty road by Marigot Bridge, it's a visual symphony of sea blue and white, with a glitter of fine crystal and a view across the water to La Belle Creole. Right on the water's edge, Le Santal is open to the breezes from its gracious formal entry to the farthest table for two on the porch.

Jean and Evelyn Dupont specialize in French cuisine and were among the first to apply its principles to local fish and produce. The Duponts have always known their worth and now seem determined to prove it. In fact, if you order wine with dinner and aren't careful, you may not escape for much under $250. Dinner only. (Telephone 87–53–48.)

If you want to pay a lot less for the same quality and creativity, try Jean Dupont's new venture by the marina in Marigot. It's called, modestly, **Jean Dupont.** (Telephone 87–71–13.)

FRENCH

Since Marigot harbors as many good restaurants and bistros as any French port town, the problem is only one of choice. Start at the waterfront, where the trio of **La Calanque, La Vie en Rose,** and **Maison sur le Port** twinkle like diamonds in a tiara around the water's edge.

As familiar as an old friend, **La Calanque** has been here over 20 years and will probably go on forever. Newly redecorated in art-deco style, its most attractive feature is the breezy, upstairs dining deck. (Downstairs seems a little stuffy but only because it's indoors.)

Entrepreneurial owner Jean Claude Coquin—who is co-owner of a number of restaurants—has changed La Calanque's menu from classic French to modified nouvelle and keeps on moving in the same direction. The beloved, bombastic "Crazy Pineapple" dessert has been supplanted by "Le Biscuit Souffle aux Fraises." Open for lunch and dinner. It's expensive, but not outrageously so. (Telephone 87–50–82.)

Just a few steps down the street, **La Vie en Rose** is an older sibling of Poisson d'Or—both owned by Roger Petit and Ray Peterson. The menus are similar, this one being, if anything, more elaborate. How about sliced breast of duck on a bed of spinach and mushrooms, covered in green-peppercorn sauce?

There's a bar and pastry shop on the ground floor, with the restaurant upstairs. In the evening, ask for a table on the porch. It's cooler out here, with romantic views of the boats in the bay.

La Vie en Rose serves lunch and dinner daily. Simpler lunches feature expertly grilled fish or light salads. Dinner costs about $110 for two. (Telephone 87–54–42.)

A little less expensive and a lot less elaborate, the colorful **Maison sur le Port** sits on a slight rise at the end of the harbor. It's pure Antillean curlique, all done up in white and plum and green—a real eye catcher. It's also one of the most popular places on the island for a lazy lunch, where you can have a salade paysanne and watch harbor happenings from the shaded porch. Open daily for lunch and dinner, with a prix fixe dinner menu at about $38. (Telephone 87–56–38.)

Less elaborate still, **Le Boucanier,** on Rue de la Liberté, has long been Marigot's favorite bistro. The comfortable, cheerful terrace overlooking the water is all done up in white and green—very primavera. The new owners specialize in grilled items, and the prices have gone from inexpensive to moderate-plus. Open daily for lunch, dinner, and Happy Hour. (Telephone 87–59–83.)

Nearby, in Rue d'Anguille's Galerie Perigourdine, **Le Nadaillac** is owned by Perigord native Fernand Malard. A longtime Caribbean resident, Malard is one of the most respected restaurateurs in the islands.

Le Nadaillac is a real production of flourishes and finery. The menu unites local seafood with the specialties from Malard's home in southwest France. In fact, there's probably not another place on the island where you can find a confit of goose. Plan on spending about $90 for two. (Telephone 87–53–77 or 87–56–16.)

L'Aventure—yet another of the Petit-Peterson restaurants—has a bright, yellow-striped awning out front, an engaging staff, a diverse culinary repertoire, and a balcony overlooking the harbor. La Belle Creole's execs ate here, watching the progress of their dream across the way, so you know it's good. Cucumber salad with fresh mint and navarin of langouste are among the specialties. This adventure will be moderately expensive. (Telephone 87–72–89.)

And finally, there's the **Mini Club.** There's no truth to the rumor that Pierre and Claudine Plessis lured Columbus ashore with a promise of the Mini Club's stuffed land crab and lobster souffle. It just seems that this popular Marigot restaurant has been there that long, serving "island French" dishes. Down a little alley across from Port La Royale, it sits on a tree-top deck, peeking at Marigot Bay between the palm fronds. Every Wednesday and Saturday, the Mini Club throws a buffet bash—$35 for all you can eat and all the wine you can imbibe, with some 35 different dishes to choose from. Open daily for lunch and dinner. (Telephone 87–50–69.)

If tiny Grand Case doesn't have as many French restaurants as big Marigot, what they have—to quote Spencer Tracy—is "cherce."

At **Rainbow,** Dutch-born Fleur Raad and partner David Henrich have created what Fleur calls the "palm-trees-porch-over-the-Caribbean atmosphere we all dreamed of when we were working in Manhattan." (She worked at Maxwell's Plum and Tavern-on-the-Green.)

Located on the waterfront side of Grand Case's miracle mini-mile, the restaurant is as bright and poetic and promising as its name. But the pot of gold may have to be in your pocket, because two of you can easily part with some $100 on a spectrum of "contemporary cooking." (Telephone 87–55–80.)

If the young, well-heeled crowd who frequent Rainbow aren't dining there, they're dining next door at **L'Escapade.** It's impeccable in every detail—prints of French sailing ships on the walls, hurricane lamps on the tables, Dover sole or sweetbreads with morels on the menu. After dinner on the porch beneath an expanse of green-and-white awning, linger for hours with a coffee and cognac. Dinner only. (Telephone 87–75–04.)

With its etched-glass entry and waterside location, **The Ritz Cafe** has become the latest "in" place on Restaurant Row—the kind of place that offers valet parking in a one-street town. The food is très chic and très cher. Open daily for lunch and dinner. Saturday brunch ($30) includes champagne. Naturally. (Telephone 87–81–58.)

Daisy's, in a red-roofed cottage by the bridge, is a fresh-faced newcomer with a lot of charm and about a dozen tables. Look for bistro food at fair prices. Prix fixe dinner is $38 for two. (Telephone 87–76–62.)

Even if every other restaurant in town is half empty, there's always a crowd waiting for one of the ten tables at **Auberge Gourmande.** Why? It's not terribly Caribbean. With brown and cream decor, it's so determinedly indoors, so French-country-inn-in-autumn, that you half expect to see a fire crackling on the hearth. But then, why not? Some restaurants just have magic. If the building is renovated Creole, the food is reliable Burgundy—escargots, frogs' legs, old-fashioned sweetbreads, lemon mousse, or apple crêpes with Calvados. Open for dinner only. Closed Wednesday. Moderately expensive. (Telephone 87–55–45.)

Cornering the neighborhood, the owners of Auberge Gourmande have opened the "contemporary French" **Le Tastevin** across the street on the water's edge. Pork in black currant sauce, *vivanneau au Porto,* and fresh sorbets are what the contemporary French are eating these days. Prices are about the same as at Auberge Gourmande. Open for lunch and dinner. Closed Wednesday. (Telephone 87–55–45.)

With a waterfront porch right next to the pier, **Le Neptune** has a big, circular bar in the front room and a slew of devoted customers. They try hard to keep prices of their "island-French" specialties down. They try hard, period. It's a nice place, and open for lunch and dinner. (Telephone 87–50–12.)

Without a lot of fanfare, little **Hevea** just keeps getting better and better. Prices for either vivanneau in a light lime sauce or pork tenderloin with mustard cream remain happily moderate. All that and Aynsley china on the ten tables. Dinner only. (Telephone 87–56–85.)

Even though it's on the "other" side of the island, Philipsburg has its share of French restaurants. Down one of Front Street's innumerable arcades (this one right next to Little Pier and the Courthouse) is **Antoine's,** decidedly French and delightfully relaxing. Local paintings hang on the white walls, and dancing lights of ships in the harbor provide a pointillist counterpoint at night.

Mushroom salad with a tangy mustard dressing makes a great starter, and Antoine's gratin—a creamy casserole stuffed with all manner of seafood and covered with bubbling hot cheese—is a treat. Try the cherries jubilee for dessert. Dinner weighs in at about $90 for two. But who wants to talk about weight? Open for lunch and dinner. (Telephone 22964.) Not content with all this, Antoine recently opened **The Red Snapper** down the street. Something to do in his spare time, as it were. A red snapper cooked in Pernod comes to $18.50. (Telephone 23834.)

Another newcomer, **Le Vaudeville at Cupecoy,** sits on a raised, open deck far above the hotel bustle. It's a pretty place, with an engaging staff and meals priced on the high end of "moderate." Among the specialties are snails with ham and garlic, lobster and veal medallions in saffron sauce, and a cloudlike kiwi mousse. Open for lunch and dinner. Closed Thursday. (Telephone 44297.)

Out on the Airport Road, **Le Perroquet** turns its back to the runway and concentrates on its better view over Simpson Bay Lagoon. It's a pretty garden restaurant in which the affable and burly chef-owner Pierre Castagné whips up outstanding French dishes. Castagné turns positively poetic when he describes the specials—breast of ostrich, filet of bison, and other wild things. Gracious Thea Langeveld keeps the place humming along at a relaxed pace. Prices are moderate to expensive. Reservations are a must. Closed Monday. Dinner only. (Telephone 44339.)

Finally, there's **Le Pavillon** out in Simpson Bay Village. The best tables are on a porch that overhangs the beach, and the French menu emphasizes local seafood. It's romantic, unpretentious, and moderately priced. (Telephone 44254.)

CREOLE

Aside from the ever-popular stuffed crab backs or occasional conch salad, Creole cooking was long the secret of the islanders, who enjoyed it in their kitchens while visitors made do with imported entrecote and frozen peas. Now out of the kitchens and on to restaurant tables, this part-African, part-Caribe Indian, part-French colonial cuisine is the hot—and sometimes scorchingly so—item on the island.

The late Yannick Le Moine and his Martinique-born wife Francillette actually started this whole Creole business some years ago when they opened Chez Lolotte in Marigot. Now at **La Rhumerie,** on a quiet back road leading to Colombier, Francillette carries on the tradition gracefully. Smoked king fish, turtle steak, spicy accras (fritters), goat curry, the best conch anywhere—the whole Creole lineup shares a menu with such noticeably French offerings as onion soup, *canard à l'orange,* and *profiteroles.*

Fairly small and quite sophisticated, **La Rhumerie** is one of the "in" places on St. Martin these days, so your chances of dropping in unannounced for dinner and finding a free table are slimmer than a saffron strand. It's well worth the $100 or so that two of you will spend on dinner. Open daily for lunch and dinner. (Telephone 87–56–98.)

As for Chez Lolotte, it's now **Cas' Anny,** an unpretentious little restaurant sitting behind pretty gardens on Rue d'Anguille. Callaloo/crab soup, lamb curry, and tortoise steak are among the most popular dishes at this moderately priced restaurant. Open daily for lunch and dinner. (Telephone 87–53–38.)

Mark is from Holland, his wife is from Guadeloupe, and between them they've created comfortable, casual **Mark's Place,** where you get huge portions of honest-to-goodness island cooking at down-to-earth prices. For about $20 (at lunch or dinner), a platter of stuffed crab backs, stuffed christophenes, blood sausage, and accras is sufficient for two modest appetites. Curried goat or conch stew with rice and beans costs even less. Timid types can have plain grilled fare. Located on Cul de Sac, this is open-to-the-breezes dining on brown tables and benches, with nifty daytime views of Pinel and Flat Islands. Reservations are a must, but they don't have a phone, so you'll have to drive down to make one in person. (Closed Monday.)

At **Chez Max,** on Rue Eboué in Marigot, the decor is eccentric (read, scruffy), but the food is island-Creole with spicy-hot pepper and vinegar on each table to add if you're brave. Great fish soup, but no credit cards. (Telephone 87–50–24.)

Up a desultory side street in sleepy Orleans, **Yvette's Restaurant** has been a fiercely guarded, cautiously whispered secret among its fans for a few years now. Motherly Yvette, who tenderizes conch with papaya leaves, knows every trick in the Creole cookbook and how to make her guests feel right at home.

The decor's not much. Eight red-clothed tables on a shiny linoleum floor, and salad-dressing bottles next to the salt shaker are the highlights. But the food is memorable. The whole Creole lineup—rice and pigeon peas, pig's ear, conch and dumplings, pork chop stew—is listed on the menu. Better yet, nibble on your complimentary johnnycakes and ask Yvette what she recommends today. Prices peak at about $20 for Yvette's cross-cultural surf 'n turf. Open daily for lunch and dinner. (Telephone 87–32–03.)

Building slowly, stone step by wooden step, simple flower pot by plastic flower pot, Philipsburg's **Harbor Lights** overlooked Bobby's Marina for years before being "discovered."

Don't be put off by the Dragon Lady facade, the Captain Kiddette mural, or the basic decor. The conch curry (or beef, or turtle) for under $10, any of the pilaus, or rotis, are the real things. Prices soar to somewhere around $12 for a West Indian shrimp scampi. It's open daily from noon to midnight, and you probably won't need a reservation. (Telephone 23504.)

If you can get together a party of four or more and if you don't mind making your plans a few days in advance, call **Madame Chance** at 87–50–45. She's been serving family-style meals in the dining room of her Grand Case home for years. This is real home cooking, the most authentic Creole anywhere—and in staggering quantities. Prices vary according to what she finds at the market, but figure on about $30 per person.

Open daily from 11 A.M. to midnight, little **Calypso**—on Airport Road—serves the Caribbean's best johnnycakes. Saltfish cakes, fried plantains, and zesty fish soup join simmering Creole specialties on the bargain-priced menu. (Telephone 44233.)

Despite an unpromising location next to Kentucky Fried Chicken on Philipsburg's Bush Road, the **Island Bar and Restaurant** is bright and sassy, serving what it calls "First Class Native Creole West Indian Food." You'll pay low prices for terrific crab backs, stewed beef with rice and peas, or conch and dumplings. (Telephone 25162.)

ITALIAN

Italian food in all its forms and many of its regional nuances is well represented on the island. **Spartaco's,** opened by La Samanna's well-loved—and former—maître d', adds a splash of sophistication to casual Cole Bay. With old statuary abounding in the Villa d'Este garden and black-and-white decor, it's like an enchanted grotto or a contessa's vacation home. Fresh pasta, veal, and seafood highlight the menu. Spartaco learned both his perfectionism and his prices at La Samanna—figure on at least $100 for two. Dinner only. (Telephone 45379.)

In Philipsburg, **DaLivio** guards the bottom of Front Street with an elegant touch of the Mediterranean. The whitewashed exterior and dark brown doors look austere, but behind them lie a warm welcome and such unexpected pleasures as lobster *fra diavolo* and homemade manicotti, plus porch-front water views. Prices are on the medium to high side, and it's open for lunch and dinner. (Telephone 22690.)

At nearby **Il Pescatore,** you can have a relatively inexpensive meal by sticking to just a tomato, mozzarella, and basil salad, or tortellini in cream sauce. Or you can run up a hefty bill by concentrating on the imaginative fish specialties—grouper baked in foil and flamed, salmon in mustard sauce, or one of the many veal dishes. Open for dinner only. (Telephone 23308.)

La Rosa Ristorante has a Liberace-style white baby grand in the corner and lovely views of Great Bay out the window. The food is southern Italian, with such offerings as rigatoni with fennel, fresh sardines, onions, raisins, tomato sauce, and cheese. Dinner only. Expensive. (Telephone 23832.)

Marigot's newest Italian restaurant, **Messalina,** is brought to you by the same folks who brought you Poisson d'Or, L'Aventure, and La Vie en Rose. It's down by the harbor; it's pretty and the food is sophisticated Italian (with island insouciance). Prices are moderate to expensive. (Telephone 87–80–39.)

On the seaside at Grand Case's southern outskirts, the moderately priced and popular **Sebastiano's** serves delicious Northern Italian food. Fresh pasta prepared daily; specialties include *ossu buco primavera.* Except for Sunday lunch, it's dinner only. (Telephone 87–58–86.)

EASTERN INFLUENCES

Asia influences **Bilboquet**—and so do the Caribbean, Wisconsin, Escoffier, and Mom. In a house on a hill in Point Blanche (just beyond the Philipsburg marinas), Robert Donn and William Ahlstrom have been turning out innovative, exciting meals utilizing local ingredients (and whatever else they can get their hands on) for over 14 years now.

Bilboquet is small—a few tables in the converted dining room—and the daily changing menu even smaller. It's a set menu, with two choices in each course. But among those choices might be chilled calabash soup, caviar torte, steamed shrimp in Thai red curry sauce, and Southern spice pie. Dinner only. Closed Monday. There's no telephone, and you must make a reservation in person 24 hours in advance. If no one's home, just leave your name on the sign-up sheet. It's fixed price at about $40 per person.

On an island first settled by Dutch traders, it's surprising there aren't more restaurants serving that ultimate potpourri of leftovers, the *rijstafel*. There is, however, **Wajang Doll.** Way down Front Street (No. 125), it's in an old West Indian house whose back wall has been removed to open onto a floodlit garden and the world's largest sea grape tree.

Owner Edu Joedhosowarno knows his onions and his spices. This is the real thing, a true Indonesian feast—satés in peanut sauce, spicy sambals, chicken in cumin, chicken in macadamia, fried bananas, shrimp crackers, and gado-gado, to name a few. Moderate prices. Dinner only, closed Sunday. (Telephone 22687.)

Tourists may overlook **Dragon Phoenix,** at the top of Back Street, but the locals don't. Some of the island's classiest restaurateurs can be seen chowing down on chow mein, jade chicken, or wor hip har. Entrée prices start at about $10 and don't go much higher. Open daily. (Telephone 22967.)

A small, garden restaurant off Marigot's Rue de Hollande, **Les Alizés** has gained a reputation as a great place to enjoy the delicate, French-influenced cuisine of Vietnam. Prices are moderate, but with its ever-growing reputation, you'll need a reservation. (Telephone 87–58–92.)

Indian restaurants have a history of short lives on this island, yet there's a new hopeful every year. This year's is **Indian Delight** in Marigot. It's good and inexpensive. (Telephone 87–53–69.)

HANGOUTS

Though half the restaurants on the island serve meals that make you want to analyze the sauces and steal the recipes, there are also hordes of "hangouts," those easygoing, amiable meeting places where the company and the conversation are more important than the food. The food is likely to be very good indeed, but it's not as distracting.

The favorite hangout for expatriate Americans, tipped-off tourists, and locals from both sides of the island is the octagonal bar festooned with plastic flowers at **Callaloo.** In Philipsburg's Promenade, it serves legendary steaks, a popular pizza, he-man hamburgers, and the reckless chicken banzai. Prices are low. From noon until the bar shuts down at 2 A.M., Callaloo acts as a kind of informal community center. If you stay long enough, you'll eventually run into everyone you wanted to see—and probably a few you didn't want to see. It's friendly, fun, and you can't miss it—there's a gaudy, purely decorative ice cream cart out front. No telephone.

Literally the oldest of St. Maarten's hangouts is Front Street's **West Indian Tavern.** A venerable cedar house with modern additions, it was built—as they insist on telling you—on the site of a centuries-old synagogue.

It's downright picturesque, with bright red hurricane shutters and doors and sign posts noting that you're 581 miles from Caracas, 3,106 miles from Los Angeles, and 5,465 miles from Kinshasha. Spilling over on to a streetside terrace, the bar has backgammon tables, peacock chairs, Balinese tikis, and a disreputable, stuffed Captain (actually more ordinary seaman) Hook propped against the piano. He is not, as is rumored, one of the former owners.

Present owner Stephen Thompson upgraded the dining room, adding on decks among the tropical trees and putting together a good Caribbean menu—charred dolphin(the fish, not the mammal), "sea symphony" with sea urchin sauce, and lots of lobster dishes peaking in the neighborhood of $30. It's a pricey tavern, and you can run up a considerable bill if you're not careful. It's open every night until midnight, with musical entertainment of one sort or another to keep things moving along. (Telephone 22965.)

Zany **Pinocchio's** combines sunny Caribbean (the locale), southern California (the owner), and sort-of Cajun (the menu). The Front Street entrance burrows through the shop-lined innards of an old cistern to an open-air terrace on Great Bay beach. There's entertainment until 2 A.M.— live music, satellite TV, and such goings-on as beer-drinking contests and the Annual Pirates and Prostitutes Ball.

The menu features pastas, jambalaya, blackened fish, and big salads. Dinner will run about $50 for two, unless you opt for the local lobster. And all this is available seven days (and nights) a week. (Telephone 22166.)

If you're looking for happy hours, piña coladas, wonder wings, and barbecued ribs, try **Zachary's.** It's up in Point

Blanche, across a hill or two from Bilboquet—and it's inexpensive. (Telephone 22260.)

Sailors, of course, have their own hangouts—places where people with Noxemad noses and salty jeans swap tales of reefs and currents and tricky winds in a clubby atmosphere. They're a lot of fun—even if you don't know a jib from a jibe.

Part of Philipsburg's Great Bay Marina complex, **Chesterfield's** has long been a favorite meeting place for both yachtsmen and imposters. No nautical hole in the wall, it's Commodore of the Fleet all the way—blue tablecloths and sea breezes, prints of mermaids on the walls, and views over some dazzling, floating tax shelters.

Whether at breakfast, lunch, or dinner, menus and prices are as light as you'd find at any self-respecting yacht club. Salade niçoise, rumaki, or club sandwiches crowd the lunch menu, all under $10. Moderately priced dinners include duck with pineapple and banana or the mermaid special of assorted seafood in puff pastry. (Telephone 23484.)

At Bobby's Marina, where serious sailors gather, the dockside **Seafood Galley** offers breakfast, lunch, dinner, and sea breezes. They've got an honest-to-goodness New England raw bar. (Telephone 23253.) **The Greenhouse** is located at the entrance to Bobby's and right on the beach. Open daily for lunch, dinner, and music. There's always a morning line of locals and day trippers picking up croissants and coffee at the breakfast bar. (Telephone 22941.)

For years, **Sam's Place,** at the top of Front Street, has been *the* spot for a hearty, it's-off-to-the-high-seas breakfast —and for a hearty lunch or dinner, too. It's breezy and come-as-you-are, with a bar up front, a fenced-in back garden, and a new second-story deck. At about 5 o'clock, sunburned sailors lope over from the marina and drop in for a drink, and the dinner crowds meander in soon after. (Telephone 22989.)

Down at Simpson Bay Lagoon (St. Maarten-side), sailors congregate at **Kim Sha,** a deceptively slap-dash bar/restaurant on the bay. The place may look ultra-casual, but it serves terrific, inexpensive Chinese food while you sit on the terrace and watch the windsurfers—or your yacht. (Telephone 45257.)

Across the road from the airport, the converted minesweeper **Lady Mariner** is now anchored in Lagoon waters. She serves light meals and respectable rum punches from 11 A.M. to 1 A.M. every day. Full dinners are served during the evening. (Telephone 42884.)

Even though it's a couple of blocks away from the water, on Marigot's Rue de la Liberté, **Davids** has a waterfront pub atmosphere—white stucco walls, dark wood trim, and all the rest. The enormous spinnaker hanging from the rafters is a dead giveaway. The restaurant is run by a some-time sailor (named David) who knows how to give other sometime sailors a pleasant evening. You'll usually find a young, trendy American crowd here. The menu features conch fritters, potato skins, macho steaks, big langoustes, and beef Wellington. Expect to pay about $65 for two. (Telephone 87–51–58.)

And if you're sailing anywhere near Grand Case, the place to meet is **The Waves**—big, breezy, fresh-paint Waves at the Grand Case Beach Club. It's the place where every-one meets to have a drink while deciding where to eat in town. In fact, they've got a restaurant right here—the only American restaurant in town. (Telephone 87–53–90.)

Captain Oliver's Marina at Hotel Captain Oliver has an Oyster Pond location, showers for sailors, custom-built yachts by the dock, reggae music on tape, and a proper, French-accented menu (local fish is the specialty) for lunch and dinner. For real hanging out, sit in one of the wooden booths with a cold Heineken and watch people messing around with boats. (Telephone 87–30–00.)

Sooner or later everyone hangs out at **Café Julianna/Club Shimaruku.** It's at the airport. You'll find people wait-ing for flights here, people waiting to meet incoming pas-sengers, people who live on the island, and a lot of people from nearby hotels who don't want to pay hotel prices for a simple hamburger or roast beef sandwich. Shimaruku (which means "wild cherry" in Papiamento) has the same convivial spirit as Callaloo, and it's owned by the same people.

These days the disco dancers hang out at **Cheri's,** in Maho's Cinnamon Grove Shopping Center. This open-air bar/restaurant serves inexpensive, casual lunches and sup-pers, then rustles up late-night snacks until 2 A.M.

After Dinner—Nightlife

With a few exceptions, nightlife on the French side consists of lingering over dinner, finishing off the wine, and considering a cognac. One of the exceptions is up the road toward Colombier (between Marigot and Grand Case), where **Night Fever's** lively bar stays open until 4 A.M. Things don't really get going there until 10 P.M. The disco at **Le Privilège** (overlooking L'Habitation and Anse Marcel) cranks up at the same time and carries on happily until dawn. In Marigot, night owls cap off an evening at **Le Piano Blanc** with a postmidnight bowl of onion soup at Bistrot Nu. Very French.

The Dutch side's big resort hotels put on weekly entertainment specials—with buffets, steel bands, limbo dancing, fire eating, and all manner of jollity. Ask at any hotel desk to find out what's happening, where, when—and how much.

Maho's **Studio 7** currently leads the disco pack, with Mullet's **Le Club** swiveling in a close second. The crowd at Mullet tends to be a little older and more sophisticated, the Maho crowd a little younger and more agile.

In Philipsburg, there are always a number of places willing to accommodate late-night revelers. **Callaloo** and **Pinocchio's** burn the midnight oil with the best of them.

But when you're talking nightlife on St. Maarten, you're really talking casinos. While the casinos are positively petite compared to the giant operations at Las Vegas or Atlantic City, they do have all the right equipment—blackjack tables, roulette wheels, craps tables, slot machines, affable dealers, and steely eyed pit managers.

With an entry right on Philipsburg's Front Street, **Rouge et Noir** is your standard storefront casino. Up the street, the St. Maarten Beach Club's **Peacock** opens for a matinee performance at 1 P.M. (It's a favorite among men who don't want to accompany their wives on shopping sprees.)

Great Bay has a reasonably serious casino, while nearby **Divi Little Bay**'s chummy, low-key casino has a much more casual, friendly kind of atmosphere. **Mullet** (the Caribbean's largest casino) and futuristic **Maho** are the fastest paced, while **Pelican** has the best view—over Simpson Bay. But since it doesn't open until 8 P.M., the view is a dubious plus. The newcomer casino at **Cupecoy/Treasure Island** boasts dealers dressed as pirates, which seems appropriate in a casino.

Casinos supposedly close at 3 A.M. If there's not much action, however, they may shut down earlier.

Sports and Sails

On this island, sporting activities are almost as popular as dining activities—a sensible combination perhaps. So far, no one has gone in for rappelling (though someone did offer hang gliding, once), but the most popular sunshine sports flourish in abundance.

The island's only golf course flourishes at Mullet Bay—and a good one it is. Designed by Joseph Lee, it's a moderately challenging course, although not challenging enough to cause apoplexy under a hot sun. Snaking right through the heart of the resort, this 18-hole lush green playground was rather miraculously built on what was once one giant sand trap. Currently, it's open only to hotel guests and to cruise-ship passengers who book in advance.

At the height of the tennis boom, nearly every hotel seemed to find some patch of land on which to scrape out at least one court, so you shouldn't have any trouble playing tennis. Your best bet again is Mullet Bay, with 14 courts—some lighted for play in the cooler evenings. The courts are open to hotel guests and outsiders alike for a fee. (Telephone 42801.)

Morning horseback rides over the hills and to the beaches leave from **Crazy Acres** every weekday. Fees are

$20 per hour, or $40 for the beach trail. (Telephone 22503, extension 201, or book through your hotel.) Out by L'Habitation, **Caid & Isa** have 8 horses for 2½-hour rides ($40) over the hills to deserted Anse de la Pomme d'Adam. (Telephone 87–32–92.)

Not surprisingly, water sports make the biggest splash on this Caribbean island. Water-skiing, windsurfing, small-boat sailing, and the currently fashionable jet-skiing are easily available on the beaches of hotels and in the waters of Simpson Bay Lagoon, where the rankest novice can get his feet wet in comfort and safety.

In St. Maarten, Little Bay's **Watersports Center** rents barracudas (water scooters) and miniature speed boats. St. Martin's **Under the Waves Watersports and Beach Stuff** at Grand Case Beach Club has an engagingly low-key surf 'n sail operation, while **St. Maarten Divers and Watersports** at the Great Bay Beach Hotel is a tad more ambitious. And on Simpson Bay Lagoon, Frik Potgieter at **Lagoon Cruises** even rents peddle boats, which he suggests as an island alternative to jogging—considerably safer under a hot sun. On the other side of the Lagoon, they're parasailing—and doing lots of other things—at **St. Maarten Watersports and Waterski Club.** (Telephone 44387.)

While the off-shore waters are not the most dramatic for scuba diving, they contain an unusual variety of tropical fish (all sizes) and one proper sunken wreck—the man-of-war *Proselyte,* which came to a sad end on a reef just outside Philipsburg's Great Bay in 1801. Today's cruise ships gingerly skirt this same reef on their way into port. Writer/photographer/diver Leroy French at **Ocean Explorers** accompanies divers on a prowl among cannons and anchors in 30-foot waters. He also guides divers through the alleys, a series of underwater caves and coral arches just off Proselyte Reef, and takes beginners to French Reef near Simpson Bay. (Telephone 45252 for rates.)

Located at Mullet Bay, **Maho Watersports** is the biggest such operation on the island, offering facilities for just about everything there is to do under, on, or in the water. Within reason, of course. Mike Myers even offers a Naui Certification Course. (Telephone 44387, or stop by any day between 9 A.M. and 4:30 P.M..)

Some of the best snorkeling on the island is on St.

Martin's north shore at Anse Marcel, a remote cove now inhabited by L'Habitation. Other than that, the favorite spots are two islands off the Atlantic coast—Pinel and Tintemarre (Flat Island). In the earlier part of the century, the latter was owned by an eccentric Dutchman who called himself the King of Tintemarre, sharing his island with 100 servants and a cotton plantation. Someone once landed a plane on the island—taking off again proved to be another matter. The only flaws in the King's paradise are the comfortable shade trees along the shore. They're manchineel trees, and their caustic, dripping sap causes painful itching and burning. In fact, a sunburn would be preferable.

Delivering passengers to these choice snorkeling areas (and to a lot of other places besides), the boats of St. Martin/St. Maarten offer picnic/snorkeling sails, destination sails, sunset sails, sightseeing sails—everything but final sales. Nearly all serve you something to eat on the trip. And this being the island that it is, you can expect something more imaginative than peanut butter sandwiches. There are probably people who choose a boat by the menu it keeps. The best places to discover your dream boat and to book space are at the **Charter Boat Center** on Little Pier in Philipsburg or at any hotel desk.

Typical of the snorkeling sails, Jerry Rosen's *Gabrielle* usually goes from Bobby's Marina to Pinel, serving refreshments on the way out. After a couple of hours of snorkeling with crew members, passengers tuck into a beach picnic that may feature Indonesian-style roast chicken. Ever the individualist, Frik Potgieter at **Lagoon Cruises** eschews local reefs, sailing the *Bluebeard* to Anguilla's Prickly Pear for a beach barbecue and the best "off-the-beach" snorkeling in these parts. Picnic/snorkeling sails cost about $60 for the day, and many boats supply underwater cameras.

For more serious fishing, **Sailfish Caraibes** at Captain Oliver's Marina sends out Bertram 33s in search of wahoo, sailfish, and blue marlin. The price—$700 a day for eight people, lunch, all equipment, and an open bar—is a good deal. What you do with a 200-pound blue marlin is up to you.

Far and away, the most popular destination to sail to is to St. Barts. Each morning, at least a half dozen boats (most of them stable catamarans) load on cases of Heinekens in preparation for the 2-hour, often choppy, crossing to Gustavia. After a few hours touring the island, everyone gets back on board for the downwind sail home, under full spinnaker and into the sunset.

One boat that handles the crossing with complete disregard for choppy seas is the stable, 75-foot *White Octopus*. The nimble young crew supplies snorkeling equipment, snacks, and drinks and gives a comprehensive briefing lecture on arrival in Gustavia. *White Octopus's* able competition includes the 60-foot *Maho*, the gold-plated *Eagle*, and the dashing, orange-hulled *El-Tigre*. All sails to St. Barts cost approximately $50 (plus the harbor tax) and most leave from one of Philipsburg's three piers.

The Style, a high-speed boat especially designed for these waters, makes the run to Saba in a little over an hour. The $45 round-trip price includes an open bar. (Telephone 22167.)

As far as sightseeing goes, *Maison Maru* is an island institution, leaving Little Pier for a trip around to Marigot for lunch and a swim in some bay, with Captain Larry Berkowitz giving a running commentary on the passing sights—a commentary that is often more amusing than accurate (around $45).

Shopping

Shopping is a consuming passion among island visitors. Even those who find this pastime just about as appealing as open heart surgery eventually succumb to one degree or another. After all, who among us doesn't relish the idea of a duty-free bargain?

Duty-free doesn't mean *free*, however. And it doesn't mean everything is a bargain. There's a lot of chaff mixed in with the wheat; but if you know what you want—from clothing to cognac—and come armed with comparison prices from home, you can easily tell if you've found a bargain. (The mind-boggling bargains down here are found during summer, when sales prices are so low they must make shop owners weep.)

While many stores have branches in resort hotels for convenience, city streets are still the best places for serious shopping. In Philipsburg, march up one side of Front Street and down the other, taking notes all the way. Detour into Old Street, a brand-new pedestrian mall lined with elegant shops. In Marigot, start at the harbor and work inland, on a broken field run through the narrow streets. Marigot's new Port La Royale complex on Simpson Bay Lagoon is a slick bargain basement for the latest sporty fashions from St. Tropez and other posh ports.

Generally speaking, shopping hours run from 9 A.M. to 6 P.M., with everyone shutting down on Sunday, and most for a leisurely couple of hours at lunchtime. When there are cruise ships in port, many Philipsburg stores stay open regardless of the day or hour. But you don't want to be there at that time.

CRYSTAL AND CHINA

Prices average an alluring 35 percent below what you'd pay in the U.S. or Canada. The names are resonantly familiar—Waterford, Lalique, Baccarat, Val St. Lambert, Wedgwood, Rosenthal—plus Royal Doulton, Copenhagen, and Worcester.

Little Switzerland, with stores in Marigot and Philipsburg (as well as on St. Thomas and St. Croix), has an extensive, top-of-the-line selection of traditional favorites. So does **Spritzer & Fuhrmann** (in Marigot, Mullet, the airport, and on East 57th Street in New York). These are not carefree Caribbean operations—Spritzer & Fuhrmann is, in fact, jeweler to the Queen of the Netherlands. They are professional operations, with an atmosphere as cool and aloof as air-conditioning.

With its main store in Marigot's Rue de la République and a branch in Philipsburg, **Oro de Sol** is the exclusive distributor for Villeroy and Boch—at savings up to 55 percent. It's also got lots of Baccarat (save about 25 percent), as well as Christofle flatware.

PERFUME AND COSMETICS

Again, there are good savings on familiar names. In Philipsburg, try **Penha** near Little Pier and at Royal Palm Plaza. It's reputable (with branches ensconced in the Netherlands Antilles since the early 1800s) and has good prices, a knowledgeable staff, and great buys on nearly anything made by Lancôme. In Marigot, **Lipstick** has an extensive selection of beauty products (especially Clarins), as well as a dazzling selection of gaudy costume jewelry. France's reliable **Printemps** is in both capitals, as is well-stocked **Maggy's.**

JEWELRY

With prices up to 30 percent less than you'd pay at home, you might as well go for the gold. There are scores of jewelry stores on Front Street, and many gold items are priced by weight. As a benchmark, start at the **New Amsterdam Store,** just down the street from the courthouse, or at **Gandelman. La Romana's** couture jewelry section has fair prices on Misani designs and an outstanding assortment of fine pieces by Italian craftsmen. Keep in mind, though that the $9,500 you shell out for a "drop dead" gold collar could also buy you a Subaru. When thinking jewelry, don't forget the redoubtable **H. Stern,** represented in St. Maarten on Front Street, or **Columbian Emeralds,** in both capitals, for a fistful of green ice.

LINENS

From hand-embroidered muffin holders to cotton terry bath sheets, linens are another good buy. In Philipsburg, try **New Amsterdam, Caribbean Palm,** and **Albert's.** Marigot's **Oro de Sol** carries Pratesi's and D. Porthault's exquisite designer sheets, towels, and tablecloths at very good savings, and **Primavera,** on Rue General de Gaulle, carries everyone else's.

CLOTHING

If you know your European designers and their worth, you can bring home some great bargains. If you don't, you can bring home some great-looking duds anyway.

In Front Street's Royal Palm Plaza and on Marigot's Rue de la République, **La Romana** has a staggering selection for men and women alike from such fashion royalty as Giorgio Armani, Fendi, and Gianfranco Ferre, with shoes by Maud Frizon. They claim you can save up to 30 percent on terrific fashions. And even in the tropical heat, the Missoni sweaters at Front Street's **Leda of Venice** look irresistible. For matching bags, **Gucci**'s boutique is just across the street.

On Old Street and out at Mullet Bay, **Java Wraps** carries sports clothes (including the bathing suit you forgot to pack) in all the splashy resort-wear colors. Surprisingly, little **New Amsterdam** has the island's largest selection of bathing suits on its second floor.

For far-out flashy, down-right punk, and a nifty line of Naf-Naf, it's **Fiorucci** in both Marigot and Philipsburg. In Port La Royal, **Raisonnable** stocks a stylish line of low-priced frocks, tops, and sweaters, while **Animale** has some wild prints, white leather jackets, and lovely laced boots just right for strolling along the beach.

Le Bastringue, in Marigot and at Mullet, carries au courant sporty fashions from France and Italy, while **Benetton** (same locations as Le Bastringue plus Front Street) carries—well, we *all* know what Benetton carries.

To complete the ensemble, pick up trendy Vuarnet sunglasses at **Optique Caraibe** (downtown Marigot and Front Street) for less than you'll pay at home.

LEATHER

For the best buys in soft Italian leather (belts, shoes, handbags, and light luggage), **MaximoFlorence** in Philipsburg's Promenade is the hands-down winner. And for inexpensive leather sandals, **The Sandal Shop** is right next door.

CARIBBEAN DESIGNS AND ART

The island produces little in the way of "native art," but you can pick up Haitian carvings or Jamaican banana-bark paintings at the Marigot market and elsewhere on the island. They look nice on a mantel.

Silk-screened fabrics by St. Thomas's Jim Tillet and St. Barts's Jean-Yves Fromant can be found at **Pierre Lapin** in Grand Case. Pierre Lapin also carries Caribee shirts from Nevis and paintings by local artists Roland Richardson and Marty and Gloria Lynn.

The Lynns also have an unofficial gallery in their house across the street. Roland Richardson's studio is in Orleans, open Thursdays from 10 A.M. to 6 P.M.

More local art decks the walls of Janet Tucker's **Coconuts,** at Great Bay Marina. It's got Haitian artwork, paintings on pieces of rum barrels, as well as beautiful cards and small gift items (starting at $2) that you can bring back to all those people you should be bringing gifts to.

Front Street's upscale **Greenwich Gallery** displays fine works by a number of Caribbean artists, and for some very good Haitian art, try Marigot's **Gingerbread Gallery,** located right by the marina. The gift shop at the new **St. Maarten Museum,** has crafts reflecting Dutch, French, African, and West Indian cultures, as well as hand-made local work.

WATCHES

These are not always a bargain, and you'd better be armed with comparison prices. Again, **Little Switzerland** and **Spritzer & Fuhrmann** are the places to start, with Philipsburg's **New Amsterdam** and **Kohinoor** worth a visit.

Generally speaking, the higher-priced watches, such as Rolex and Patek Philippe, will be the best bargains, with little savings on lower-priced time pieces. At **Oro de Sol,** a Piaget Polo costs about half what it does at home. That's still a lot. They've also got a good line of Ebel—those super-slim Swiss sports watches—and Cartier at the same stratospheric savings.

CAMERAS, RADIOS, STEREO EQUIPMENT

If you live near discount centers in a major city, buy these at home. However, the East Indians of Front Street—**Ram's, Boolchand, Kohinoor,** and **Gulmohar**—are highly competitive and willing to bargain. What's more, they're all reputable and clustered together near Little Pier.

LIQUOR

You can bring one liter per person back into the States, but savings are such that you might want to bring back more. Even paying the duty, you'll come out ahead. Heavenly, 10-year-old Martinique rum is sold in Marigot supermarkets for about $8 a quart. Rémy Martin goes for about $20.

The island's most extensive wine selection can be found on Marigot's Rue de la Liberte. Only the best French is sold by bottle or case in an atmosphere as cool as a wine cellar. For lesser spirits, stick to the supermarkets with their low, low prices.

Guavaberry liqueur, a mildly intriguing concoction, whose base is rum and guavaberries, is a local "Grandma's recipe" drink now being produced in some quantity. It hasn't quite caught on as the national drink, but it makes an interesting souvenir. Available nearly everywhere, it costs about $15 a bottle.

ISLAND SOUVENIRS

Souvenirs are everywhere. For a super selection, try **Gem Palace,** tucked among the fancy shops of Rue de la Republique. The great big umbrellas with painted wooden handles ($9.95), straw hats ($8.50), and an enormous collection of T-shirts may add up to the best bargain on the island.

LAST CHANCE

If there's *anything* you forgot to buy, from T-shirt to tiara, you can get it somewhere among the airport's 26 shops.

CUSTOMS INFORMATION

If you decide to partake in some of the island's shopping delights, you should be aware of what you can take home before you have to start paying duty. U.S. residents may bring home $400 worth of foreign merchandise for personal use (provided you've been out of the country for at least 48 hours and have made no similar claims in the previous 30 days), plus one liter of alcohol (over age 21 only), 100 non-Cuban cigars, 200 cigarettes, and one bottle of perfume trademarked in the U.S. After that, you are going to pay a 10% tax on the next $1,000 worth of goods.

Canadian residents are entitled to a $150 per year customs exemption. In addition, they can bring in 50 cigars, 200 cigarettes, 2 lbs. of tobacco, and 40 oz. of liquor duty free. For further details, get a copy of the Canada Customs brochure, *I Declare*.

British subjects can bring home 200 cigarettes or 100 cigarillos or 50 cigars or 250 grams of tobacco, two liters of table wine plus one liter of alcohol over 22% proof or two liters of alcohol under 22% proof or two more liters of table wine, 50 grams of perfume or ¼ liter of toilet water, in addition to other goods up to the value of £32.

Island Excursions

The four surrounding islands are as different from one another as they are from St. Martin/St. Maarten—and that's very different indeed. They're all tiny, with distinct personalities: Anguilla is flat, sandy, and pure distilled Caribbean; St. Barts is pretty, precise, and markedly French; Saba is mountainous and lush, a Shangri-la surrounded by water; and Statia (St. Eustatius) is remote, undeveloped, and caught in a time warp.

Day trips to the islands are easy to arrange, and if you can't see all there is to see in a day, you can sample selectively—finding plenty of reasons to return.

Anguilla

Exploring

Quiet and still relatively unspoiled, Anguilla is the archetypal Caribbean island. Innumerable white-sanded beaches and coves are scattered around its limited perimeter. Small islets with palm trees lie not far offshore. The island is ringed by reefs and the sunburning backs of snorkelers. The waters are aquamarine and the pace is snail-like.

Just off St. Martin's north coast, Anguilla is easily accessible for a day's outing of beaches, seafood, and total peace. Ferries make the 17-minute run between Marigot and Blowing Point frequently during the day ($8 one way, plus harbor taxes at both ends), and some offer evening service ($10) so you can tarry through dinner. WINAIR flies from Juliana to Wallblake Airport three times a day. It's a seven-minute flight and costs about $30 for a round-trip ticket. Add on a $5 departure tax from St. Maarten and a $3 tax from Anguilla.

Taxis will be waiting and willing at both airport and pier, and a 2½-hour island tour costs about $40. Or you can tour on your own. Connor's Car Rental (telephone 2433) has cars for about $35 a day, and they'll handle the minor formalities of a local driver's license ($8). As befits an outpost of the British Empire, driving is on the left.

Seized by a fit of unaccustomed whimsy, Columbus named the island "the eel" when he first caught sight of this 17-mile-long, 3-mile-wide sliver of flat island. Flat indeed—only small hillocks poke up behind the sea grape trees lining the beaches. It's not lush, either. Scrub pines and stands of tamarind trees are interspersed with the occasional cascade of flowering pink coralita and puffs of dust.

Anguillans have never been much into horticulture, however, preferring to concentrate on the sea. This has always been a nation of boat builders, fishermen, and lobster trappers. Boat racing is the major sport on the island. The picturesque Anguillan boats—deep-hulled, Marconi-rigged sloops—are unique in the world except for, unaccountably, some kindred craft in remote corners of Indonesia.

DINING: THE NORTHWESTERN SHORE

Way up on the northwestern shore, Island Harbour is the seafaring center of the island—and the local lobster bin. Fishing boats line the beaches, and it's very scenic—espe-

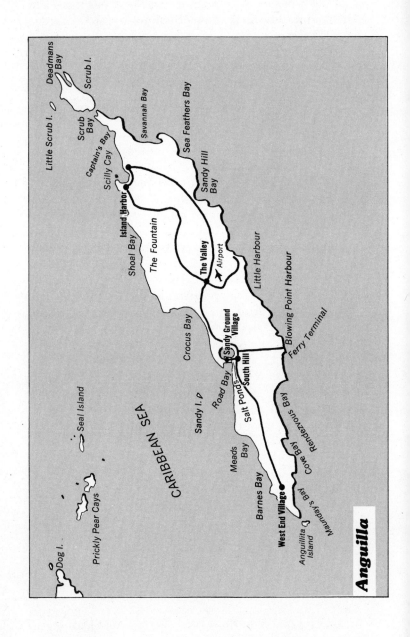

Anguilla

cially if you're into boat building. The new owners of **The Fish Trap Restaurant** spot the fishermen as they're coming in and get the pick of the catch. The palm-frond roof is quintessentially Caribbean, but the cooking is French. Open daily for lunch and dinner. It's quite expensive—and entirely worth it. (Telephone 4488.)

For visitors, however, the prime activity is not boat building, but beach hunting—searching for the ultimate strip of sand. All 30 beaches are pretty wonderful, and some are so deserted that if you see a set of footprints, you think they must belong to Robinson Crusoe's Friday. Reefs behind the reefs make for ideal snorkeling conditions at Shoal Bay. And at **Happy Jack's** beach bar, you can rent flippers and masks for an hour's snorkeling before settling down to a rum punch and lobster salad.

At Crocus Bay, diving pelicans put on their Kamikaze aerial displays, which you can watch from the porch at **Roy's** while having some honest-to-goodness Yorkshire fish 'n chips. Open daily. (Telephone 2470.) And down at the southwest end of the island (the tail of the eel), Rendezvous, Maunday, and Mead's Bay each have their champions when it comes to "most beautiful beach" awards.

LODGING

At Mead's Bay, the ultra-glamorous **Malliouhana Hotel** sits in rough-around-the-edges Anguilla like a diamond in a bowl of granola. (Despite its Hawaiian ring, "Malliouhana" was the original Carib name for the island.) Guests here pay diamond prices for their privileges, but you can pay a mere handful of gold for a French-accented lunch. As an option, head for Barnes Bay (the beach next door) and a spectacular buffet lunch by the pool at **Coccoloba**. Surely *everyone* knows by now that Coccoloba is a former health spa. As a third option, have a slimming salad and the "Devil Made Me Do It" chocolate mousse at Pimm's, the seaside restaurant at the captivating **Cap Juluca** on Maunday's Bay. That's three diamonds in a row.

After the beaches, Malliouhana, Coccoloba, and Cap

Juluca, the rest of the island's sights can be run down fairly
quickly. The Valley, Anguilla's prosaically named capital, is
a sleepy village with government buildings, a seemingly
deserted off-shore banking complex, and a couple of worthy
local restaurants.

DINING: SANDY GROUND VILLAGE

At Sandy Ground Village, a small strip of land—little
more than a beach and a back road—separates the Salt Pond
from deep Road Bay. Cargo ships pull up at the long pier,
and visiting yachts pull in and out of the harbor. Casual
restaurants— **Riviera, Johnno's Fish Pot,** and **The Barrel
Stay,** among others—serve unpretentious meals in a barefoot atmosphere. Sunday afternoon is party time at Johnno's. Reggae and calypso music are played by a band on the
beach. For real, down-home Anguillan cooking, climb up
South Hill to **Lucy's Harbour View.** Lucy is not much for
fancy decor—plants grow in paint cans and mix-and-match
tables dot the terrace, along with folding chairs with cush-
ions that have launched a thousand seats. But she's got a
welcoming smile and a deft hand with curries and fish.
Prices for everything from curried conch to grilled lobster
are moderate. Closed Tuesday evening. (Telephone 6253.)

If you've got only one stop in Sandy Ground, however,
stroll down the strand to **The Mariners,** a friendly, low-key
hotel perfect for Anguilla and for feeling right at home. It's
West Indian style personified—open to the breezes, with
gingerbread trim, and right on the beach. It's also something of a hangout for island visitors, with people swapping
beach stories in the bar, then staying on for Anguillan fish
soup or grilled crayfish with hollandaise. Prices are moderate. Open daily. (Telephone 2671.)

Sandy Ground is also the local water-sports center.
Tamariain Watersports rents all manner of boats and flippers, and for a small fee will take you over to Sandy Island—
a palm-treed island where the snorkeling is sublime. If you
get there early enough or late enough in the day, you'll have
this little Paradise all to yourself.

Even Paradise has a small beach bar and barbecue on

it, however. In the past couple of years, nearly every other stretch of sand seems to be sprouting a restaurant. At Little Harbour, **Cinnamon Reef Beach Hotel** has a small beach, a huge swimming pool, and a pleasant restaurant with bay views and an American accent. Lunch is about $30 for two. (Telephone 2727.) The **Ferry Boat Inn Restaurant** near Blowing Point serves burgers and local surf 'n turf on an open porch, where you can watch the coral shore by day and St. Martin's lights by night. (Telephone 6613.) On the main road near The Valley, Keith Harrigan's **Old House** features "potfish" and other Anguillan dishes in a colonial manor house complete with Ionic columns. (Telephone 2228.)

Aside from the comic-opera Bay of Piglets (when British troops invaded the island upon its refusal to become independent), Anguilla has never been much in the news. With the current boom of new hotels and restaurants, however, the quiet days may soon be gone forever.

ST. EUSTATIUS

EXPLORING

Nobody calls it St. Eustatius but cartographers, scholars, and strangers—and no one remains a stranger for long on little Statia. It's a friendly, slow-paced island, where everyone "hails up" everyone else, kinfolk and visitor alike. Donkeys often outnumber cars on the narrow roads, and sprays of yellow buttercups or orange profusions of Pride of Barbados are a cause for small celebration.

It's not much as islands go—12 square miles, a string of black sand beaches, two mountains with a plain between them, and one town. But what it lacks in high-rises, it makes up in history. In the 17th-century heyday of the Dutch West Indies trading companies, Statia was a neutral free port known as The Golden Rock. It was a haven for merchants, shipping magnates, smugglers, and anyone with a mind to buy or sell. It was also the first nation in the world to salute

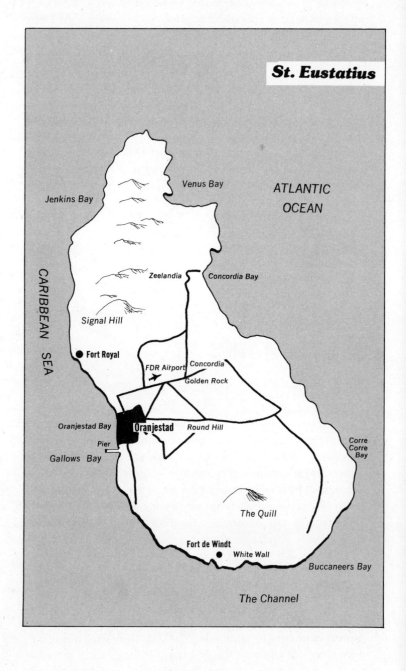

St. Eustatius

ATLANTIC OCEAN

Venus Bay

Jenkins Bay

CARIBBEAN SEA

Zeelandia

Concordia Bay

Signal Hill

Fort Royal

FDR Airport

Concordia

Golden Rock

Oranjestad Bay

Oranjestad

Round Hill

Pier

Corre Corre Bay

Gallows Bay

The Quill

Fort de Windt

White Wall

Buccaneers Bay

The Channel

the new American flag in 1776—a friendly, if ill-considered, act for which it paid a high price.

Just 48 miles south of St. Maarten, Statia's Franklin Delano Roosevelt Airport can be reached by WINAIR on its daily "commuter" runs among the islands. The fare is about $40 for a round-trip ticket, and a direct flight takes 20 minutes.

Virginia Tours Historic Sightseeing Expeditions offers 2½-hour tours ($10 per person) that give you the lowdown on the highlights. You can also rent a car at the airport from $30 a day. The Tourist Information Office at the airport will be glad to help.

Oranjestad will be your first destination. Statia's capital (and only town), Oranjestad was, 200 years ago, one of the richest towns in the world. It was here, from the ramparts of seemingly impregnable Fort Oranje, that the salute to the American flag came. And it was here that irate British Admiral George Romney came some five years later to sack the town, blow up the breakwater that protected it, and flood the entire lower half of Oranjestad. Using some such excuse as "lack of adequate staffing," the Dutch general didn't defend the fabulous fort.

Fort Oranje has been carefully reconstructed (the main Tourist Office is located next door), and from its impregnable ramparts you can get a good view of the old foundations and breakwater under the waves. Not far away is the roofless shell of the old Dutch Reform Church, surrounded by graves of colonial heroes and scoundrels, as well as generations of Statians. The tower has been restored, and a climb up the narrow stairs will reward you with grand views of the old town, of nearby Saba, and nearly all Statia for just a small donation to the Historical Society. Down a nearby dusty side street stands the equally roofless Honen Dalim, the second oldest synagogue in the Western Hemisphere.

Otherwise, Oranjestad is today an exceedingly quiet town, whose center is alternately called "the wide place in the road" or "three widows corner" and where two cars meeting constitutes a traffic jam. The loudest sound is the ruckus of children in the schoolyard or the occasional squeal of excitement from one of the archaeological teams who "dig" the island.

DINING

The most excitement in Oranjestad is down in the old town, where benches and flowering bougainvillea make up a small park. There's a nice beach for swimming and, improbably, one of the Caribbean's best small hotels. Surrounded by (and built on) the old foundations, **The Old Gin House** is the creation of Americans John May and Marty Scofield. Furnished with antiques, Haitian art, and nautical salvage, the hotel is a mix of formal (the dining room) and barefoot casual (a breakfast/cocktail patio perching precariously over the rocky beach and more ruins). Some rooms overlook a pool, part of the dining room, and masses of tropical blossoms. Other rooms overlook the blasted breakwater and—in the distance—Saba.

The kitchen here was one of the first in the Caribbean to utilize local ingredients in sophisticated dishes. Pernod-flavored lobster, "Antillian" ham glazed with papaya sauce, and stuffed crab backs (the crabs lured out at night in an adaptation of flashlight tag) are some of the specialties. Lunches are less exotic—and less expensive. (Telephone 2319.)

The best choice for lunch on a day trip may be **Maison sur la Plage** on deserted Zeelandia Bay—just a hop, skip, and donkey ride from Oranjestad. This French import has become so totally Statian that after a fresh salad and some local fish, you may be tempted to snooze by the pool, dreaming about new friends and old tales. (Telephone 2256.)

Old tales are important, for every inch of the island has a story. At English Quarter, now no more than a tangle of overgrown underbrush, the vain General Cornwallis had his riding track. On a sunny afternoon in 1785, he summoned all his troops to admire his equestrian skills. On the same afternoon, the Dutch and French were busy invading the other side of the island, which they captured without a shot.

ST. BARTS

EXPLORING

A small jewel of an island, St. Barts (or St. Barthélemy, or St. Barths) lies just 15 miles southeast of St. Maarten. Not exactly standard sandy Caribbean, it's elegant and expensive, sophisticated and *sauvage*, and thoroughly French. It's exclusive, too. With a tiny, impossible-to-expand airport, a harbor more suited to catamarans than cruise ships, and a moratorium on building, it's likely to remain all that.

St. Barts's eight square miles contain pretty little villages, beautiful people, and beautiful beaches. Some are rough (beaches, not people) with Atlantic surf, some smooth, and some nearly inaccessible except by boat or overland hikes. And despite its manicured grace, the island is also angular, with steep roads and hairpin turns suited only to utility vehicles, goats, and French drivers practiced in insouciance.

In addition to the armada of day sailers coming from St. Maarten (see *Sports and Sails*), WINAIR (Windward Island Airways) flies over three times each day and Air St. Barthélemy five times daily. The flights take 10 minutes and cost about $50 round-trip. Air Guadeloupe also flies here from Grand Case's Espérance. If you fly from Juliana, there's a $5 departure tax, and a $3 St. Barts departure tax coming back.

Taxis and mini-buses depart from the airport for one-hour tours of the island. Figure on about $15 per person. If you want to explore on your own, rent a stick-shift Mini-Moke. The rate is about $40 a day, and they honor foreign licenses. St. Barth Car Rental (aka Avis, telephone 27–71–43) and a host of others are right at the new airport.

Although you can't see all St. Barts in one day, you can make a start. Start at the capital, Gustavia—whose distinctly Swedish name is the result of a little financial wheeling and dealing between the Swedish and French governments in past centuries. The town curls around the U-shaped harbor, where enviable yachts bob up and down. Sturdy, stone buildings nudge up close to the waterfront, and small West

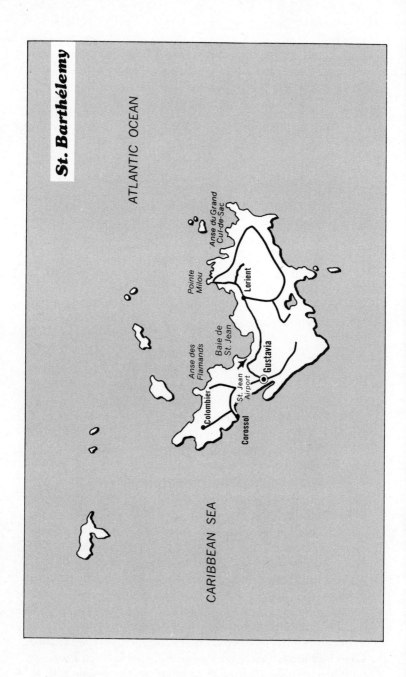

St. Barthélemy

ATLANTIC OCEAN

Anse du Grand
Cul-de-Sac

Pointe
Milou

Lorient

Anse des
Flamands

Baie de
St. Jean

Gustavia

St. Jean
Airport

Colombier

Corossol

CARIBBEAN SEA

Indian homes climb the hills behind. Going about its business quietly, Gustavia is a town of small cafés and duty-free
boutiques, all no more than a few steps away from one
another. Compared to St. Martin/St. Maarten, shopping is
negligible, but it's certainly more relaxing.

Not far from the picturesque ruins of Swedish army
barracks, **La Marine Service** (27–70–34) is the local water-
sports center. It and **Yacht Charter Agency** (27–62–38)
send graceful, two-masted ketches around the island to see
those inaccessible beaches, serving graceful French lunches
on the way.

DINING

Gustavia's pace is conducive to pausing in mid-stroll
and considering what to do next—or watching other people
do the same thing. People do this a lot at **Le Select,** a corner
bar with loud music, plastic tables, a framed needlepoint
saying "Valkommen," T-shirts hanging from the rafters,
and a large picture of a Norsk lady being nuzzled by a
reindeer. In accents and atmosphere, it's a truly international hangout.

Just across the street, the terraced café **L'Oubli** is just
as convivial, if a bit more restrained. And the menu is pure
French bistro, with superb omelets and bowls of hearty
onion soup at restrained prices.

Gustavia dining choices range from the open-air interi-
or gardens of **La Crémaillère** (lobster thermidor is the specialty) on Rue du General de Gaulle to the second-floor
balcony of **Au Port,** on the harbor's edge. Both are expensive.

For an evening drink (or an expensive French meal),
Hotel Hibiscus sits high on a hill overlooking the frenzy of
greater downtown Gustavia. The views are delightful, and
so is the quiet. Sometimes, the loudest sound around is
likely to be the crow of a rooster.

Even farther up the hills behind the town—at the top
of Morne Lurin to be precise—the exclusive, exquisite
Castelets looks down on the entire world. Reclusive film
stars and millionaires hide away in its 10 rooms, but its

views, its grotto bar, and its deservedly famous restaurant are open to everyone. Lunch is about $75 for two; dinners may be a tasty $150. Reservations are a must.

West of Gustavia, the harbor town of Corossol steps right out of another time—Brigadoon on St. Barts. The women still wear high, starched bonnets ("quichenottes"), which date back to 17th-century Normandy, and the towns-people view the 20th century only out of the corners of their eyes. Stow your camera—the locals won't be photographed. They will, however, be glad to sell you woven straw place mats, baskets, and hats.

Even a two-hour visit to St. Barts must include a visit to fashionable St. Jean Bay—the place to see and be seen. A string of small hotels share a silver strip of beach that starts at the airport runway and ends at the rocky fortress of Eden Rock, the island's first hotel. Start with a drink in the bar at **Emeraude Plage** and a game of backgammon in the "games corner." Have another drink on the pool deck at **Filao Beach,** under baskets of colorful plastic flowers, where flags of three nations snap in the breeze, and dashing bartenders mix up powerful concoctions in a blender. Have yet another at the optimistically named **St. Jean Beach Club.** It looks like a beachfront diner—you half expect to see a Coca-Cola sign on top—but they make the best piña colada on the island.

No visit to St. Jean Bay (or to St. Barts for that matter) is considered complete without lunch at **Chez Francine.** Find a table under one of the thatched umbrellas on the deck, place your order, then skip down the steps for a short preluncheon swim. It's obviously rather informal here. Simple lunches on a wooden platter—grilled chicken/steak/fish, a mountain of *pommes frites*, and a garden of salad—will come to about $50 for two.

At lunchtime, **Pelican** plays a casual noonday theme—simple garden lunches on long, cafeteria-like tables, with three blue-and-gold parrots observing all from the branches of a micalpa tree. Pelican dinners served inside the pretty seaside home get more serious (as in serious hare breast with peppercorn sauce) and more expensive—about $100 for two.

The long flight of wide steps leading up to **La Loui-**

siane gives it the air of a small palace owned by some scion of a minor royal family. The cuisine is creative (grouper poached in lettuce leaves and the like), and the breezy dining terrace just plain delightful. You'll need a reservation, (27–71–36), and since it's open for dinner only, you'll have to stay overnight on St. Barts. Is that such a bad idea?

Even on a short trip to the island, it's worth a detour from the "cities" to see the new **Manapany Cottages** on Anse des Cayes. You may not want to swim in these choppy, coral-infested waters, but you'll want to lunch at a table by the side of the pool at Manapany's casual restaurant, Ouanalao.

Way out at Grand Cul de Sac, **Guanahani**—the latest in local luxury—has an expensive, white-glove restaurant open for dinner only. It also boasts a chic outdoor café, **L'Indigo,** for lunches and beachfront dinners. Who wants to be indoors anyway?

A few sunny steps down the strand, **El Sereno Beach Hotel** is, in many ways, the *ne plus ultra* of local hotels. It's elegant, French, and quintessentially St. Barts, filled with blinding white walls, royal blue lampposts, palm trees rampant, and a tiled swimming pool (with islands, yet) on a deck by the dining room. At night little lights twinkle up from beneath the deck floor. If Chez Francine is *the* place for lunch, Sereno could claim to be *the* place for dinner.

Owners Marc and Christine Llepez and the rest of the crew hail from Lyons—gastronomic capital of the world. In this glittery setting, the clever chefs effortlessly toss off simple little dishes, such as lobster ravioli in cabbage butter with truffle slices or wine-macerated fruits blanketed by soufflés. The whole exercise will cost you about $150 for two. (Telephone 27–64–80.)

Next door, **Club Lafayette** serves expensive lunches at what amounts to a glorified beach bar. But it's one of *the* places to be seen, and that's important on St. Barts.

SABA

EXPLORING

Of all the neighboring islands, tiny Saba—28 miles south of St. Maarten—may be the most enchanting. It is often compared to Bali Hai. It is also compared to Shangri-la, Napoleon's hat, or even a green gum drop. From the sea, it looks like a moss-covered rock, rising from the water and wreathed with a tiny crown of cloud. From the air, it looks— sure enough—like a green gum drop.

Saba is that rarity in the Caribbean—an island with absolutely no beaches. It is five square miles of awesome cliffs and deep ravines, of mini-hamlets and tidy homes, of lush tropical vegetation, and an abundant amount of charm.

Windward Island Airways' (WINAIR) precision-landing planes pop on and off the runway (which resembles an accidental flat spot on a hilltop) at Juancho E. Yrausquin Airport several times a day. The flight from St. Maarten takes 17 minutes and costs $45 round trip.

On Saba, mini-buses give 2½-hour tours of the island "through all four villages." The cost is $7 per person ($30 for a group of four).All the drivers are authentic "characters," so the tours are great fun.

The airport and Fort Bay (the main port, where a blanket-sized patch of sand is the island's closest approximation of beach) anchor either end of Saba's nine-mile-long road. After "experts" said the road couldn't be built, it was hand-built by locals under the direction of a man with a mail-order diploma in engineering. Strung like beads along the impossible road are colorfully named towns such as Lower Hell's Gate, The Bottom, and Booby Hill. Photographers snap away happily at gingerbread houses with red-shingled roofs and intricately carved eaves. Marigolds, orchids, and striped crotons bloom in the gardens; bougainvillea spills over garden walls and back toward gravestones in the side yard. (Since five-square-mile islands are not conducive to expansive cemeteries, Sabans have traditionally buried departed ancestors in the garden.)

Despite the lack of beaches, Saba does offer some fine

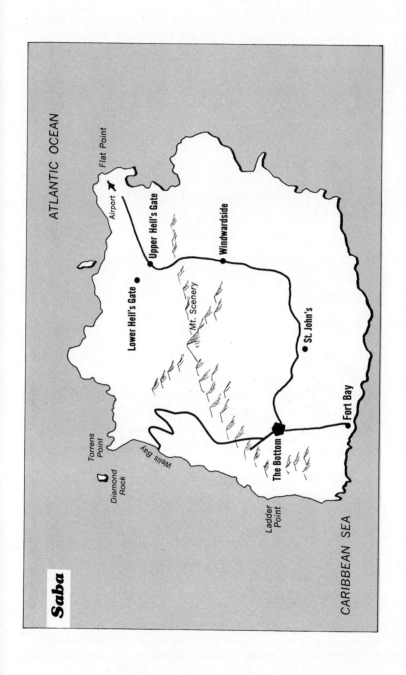

scuba diving. Carolyn Buchanan at **Saba Deep** (telephone 3347) and Lou Bourque at **Sea Saba** (telephone 2246) supply all equipment, give lessons, and offer remarkable dives past underwater mountain pinnacles and through forests of elkhorn coral in the newly established Marine Park.

Saba also offers some fine mountain climbing, up Mount Scenery, all 2,855 feet of it, to the highest point in the Antilles. The sometimes slippery climb up 1,064 rough-hewn steps slithers past breadfruit trees, groupings of lemon trees, and giant ferns to a mahogany grove at the cloud-covered top. The climb takes a couple of hours—and coming down is harder than going up.

Mostly, however, visitors poke around the fairy-tale towns with their enchanting names. Saba's capital, The Bottom, sits very high up in what is reputed to be the crater of an extinct volcano. Narrow, winding streets meander past the Lieutenant Governor's mansion, a 200-year-old Anglican Church, and the new Administration Building, built to resemble an old Colonial Administration Building.

The Bottom is home to **Saba Artisans Foundation,** where bright prints of hibiscus flowers, cassava leaves, and other local flora are silk-screened onto sturdy cotton, then fashioned into clothing and accessories. The finished products are sold in the adjoining showroom (Monday through Friday), at the airport, and in local gift shops. The foundation also has a fine selection of T-shirts, some emblazoned with the newly-designed Saban coat of arms. The epaulets depict the "Famous Saba Cabbage."

Silk-screening is, in a way, an updating of Saba's traditional handicraft—delicate, drawn-thread needlework known as Saba lace. Tablecloths, shirts, napkins, pillow cases, and other examples of this ornamental embroidery can be found everywhere on the island. The **Island Craft Shop** has a good selection, but it's more interesting to purchase your Saba lace from the lady who made it right in her own living room or from one of the "cooperatives," staffed by those same ladies.

Saba's other popular export is Saba Spice, a homemade liqueur with a distinctive, exotic bouquet. Suffice it to say that it's based on rum and fennel, with 11 other secret ingredients—the secrets of which are passed from mother to daughter. Suffice it also to say that one bottle lasts a long time.

Windwardside is Saba's other major town, clinging to the edge of a hill in the shadow of Mount Scenery. Here you'll find most of the island gift shops (one sign reads "Gifts—Oddments—Pretties") and most (two) of the island's hotels.

DINING

Captain's Quarters—once the home of a Saban sea captain—is an idyllic retreat. The spacious, airy rooms (Queen Beatrix slept here) have hurricane shutters, antique furnishings, and ceiling fans. A cliffside pool is flanked by a gazebo and a lively bar. Meals are served in a cool dining verandah shaded by "walls" of vine-draped breadfruit and mango trees, of palm fronds and elephant ears. Captain's Quarters is where most people stop for lunch on a day trip to the island. The top price: $16 for lobster. (Telephone 2201.)

Up the hill a bit, **Scout's Place** ("Bed 'n Board, Cheap 'n Cheerfull") has a dramatic view over the Saban hills to the sea from its dining terrace. Another former government guest house, Scout's Place is a local hangout, a great place for a rum punch at sunset, and it's an island institution. After many years, Scout's has added a pool and a few more rooms. Ah, progress! Lunches—sandwiches, fish, chicken, steak—run about $10 per person. (Telephone 2205.)

The newest entry in Saba's "gourmet sweepstakes," **Guido's Place,** is a pizza restaurant with a snack bar in front, a sit-down dining room, and a back terrace for disco dancing. Not far from Scout's Place, it's an interesting addition to the town.

And that's it. That's Saba—where mangoes fall in the street, iguanas sun themselves on stone walls, bumblebees hum hymns in the graveyards, and time stands still.

Index

Fodor's Travel Guides

U.S. Guides

Alaska
Arizona
Atlantic City & the
  New Jersey Shore
Boston
California
Cape Cod
Carolinas & the
  Georgia Coast
The Chesapeake Region
Chicago
Colorado
Dallas & Fort
  Worth

Disney World & the
  Orlando Area
Florida
Hawaii
Houston &
  Galveston
Las Vegas
Los Angeles, Orange
  County, Palm Springs
Maui
Miami, Fort Lauderdale,
  Palm Beach
Michigan, Wisconsin,
  Minnesota

New England
New Mexico
New Orleans
New Orleans *(Pocket
  Guide)*
New York City
New York City *(Pocket
  Guide)*
New York State
Pacific North Coast
Philadelphia
The Rockies
San Diego
San Francisco

San Francisco *(Pocket
  Guide)*
The South
Texas
USA
Virgin Islands
Virginia
Waikiki
Washington, DC
Williamsburg

Foreign Guides

Acapulco
Amsterdam
Australia, New Zealand,
  The South Pacific
Austria
Bahamas
Bahamas *(Pocket
  Guide)*
Baja & the Pacific
  Coast Resorts
Barbados
Belgium & Luxembourg
Bermuda
Brazil
Britain *(Great Travel
  Values)*
Budget Europe
Canada
Canada *(Great Travel
  Values)*
Canada's Atlantic
  Provinces
Cancún, Cozumel,
  Mérida, the
  Yucatán
Caribbean

Caribbean *(Great
  Travel Values)*
Central America
China
China's Great Cities
Eastern Europe
Egypt
Europe
Europe's Great Cities
Florence & Venice
France
France *(Great Travel
  Values)*
Germany
Germany *(Great Travel
  Values)*
Great Britain
Greece
The Himalayan
  Countries
Holland
Hong Kong
Hungary
India, including Nepal
Ireland
Israel

Italy
Italy *(Great Travel
  Values)*
Jamaica
Japan
Japan *(Great Travel
  Values)*
Jordan & the Holy Land
Kenya, Tanzania,
  the Seychelles
Korea
Lisbon
Loire Valley
London
London *(Great Travel
  Values)*
London *(Pocket Guide)*
Madrid & Barcelona
Mexico
Mexico City
Montreal &
  Quebec City
Munich
New Zealand
North Africa
Paris

Paris *(Pocket Guide)*
Portugal
Rio de Janeiro
The Riviera *(Fun on)*
Rome
Saint Martin &
  Sint Maarten
Scandinavia
Scandinavian Cities
Scotland
Singapore
South America
South Pacific
Southeast Asia
Soviet Union
Spain
Spain *(Great Travel
  Values)*
Sweden
Switzerland
Sydney
Tokyo
Toronto
Turkey
Vienna
Yugoslavia

Special-Interest Guides

Bed & Breakfast
  Guide: North America
Health & Fitness
  Vacations

Royalty Watching
Selected Hotels of
  Europe

Selected Resorts
  and Hotels of the U.S.
Shopping in Europe

Skiing in North
  America
Sunday in New York